ASK NOT

WHAT YOUR COUNTRY

CAN DO FOR YOU—

ASK WHAT YOU CAN DO

FOR YOUR COUNTRY.

John F. Kennedy

PICTORIAL ENCYCLOPEDIA

Volume 16

1957 to 1966

Space Supremacy And Freedom

Dramatically pictured with new living art and stirring narrative in a series of authoritative volumes to enrich the interest and appreciation of young Americans in their heritage of freedom and equality

Of AMERICAN HISTORY

SPECIAL CONSULTANTS

Bernard S. Miller, ED.D.
Associate Director, John Hay Fellows Program; Collaborator with James B. Conant, *The American High School Today.*

Kenneth W. Lund, PH.D.
Superintendent Oak Park-River Forest High School, Oak Park, Illinois; Chairman, North Central Association Committee on Guidance and Counseling.

Kenneth L. Peters, M.S.
Superintendent of Schools, Beverly Hills Unified School District, Beverly Hills, California.

CONTRIBUTORS

Daniel Powell, M.A.
Teacher, Social Studies Dept., Senn High School, Chicago; John Hay Fellow, University of Chicago.

Commander William M. McCarthy
United States Naval Reserve; Formerly Officer in Charge Press Section Public Information, Navy Department, Washington, D.C.

Pearl J. Slaton, M.A.
Formerly Teacher Public Elementary Schools, McKinley High School, Chicago; Reader, Niles Township High School, Skokie, Illinois.

Earl Schenck Miers
HISTORICAL EXPERT AND AUTHOR.

Jerry Wolfert
HISTORIAN AND AUTHOR.

ILLUSTRATORS and GRAPHIC ARTS

Clarence B. Pontius • Richard Potts • Charles R. McCurry • Robert Caples • Bill Law • William Gray • Charles Spears • Steve Dobson • Geraldine A. Simkus • Alexander Toth • Ray Vinella • Gail Pinchot • J. M. LaGrotta • George Bures • Robert Boehmer • Jim Gindraux • Don Simmons • Si Mezerow • Arnie Kohn •

UNITED STATES HISTORY SOCIETY, INC.

The Widening Struggle

Going into the late 1950's, the world was engaged in struggles in all directions—including upward to outer space!

Grim earth-bound contests were in progress in Europe, Africa, the Middle East and Far East . . . soon the race for supremacy would extend into the far reaches of the universe!

Basically, the over-all struggle was a Cold War between Democracy and Communism. Specifically, it was between the United States and the Soviet Union, leaders in the conflict of creeds.

Democracy and Communism had engaged in a bloody armed clash in Korea during 1950 and 1953. This was called a "police action," but it cost the lives of 33,629 Americans in battle.

In Europe, the question of Germany was far from settled. The Western powers wanted Germany to be unified through free elections by the people. The Soviet Union, having formed a puppet government in East Germany, demanded a "free and demilitarized" Berlin. This, the West contended, would expose all of Berlin to seizure by the East German Communists—and that would lead to an all-Communist Germany.

The controversy reached a peak from June, 1948, to May, 1949, when the Soviets sealed off West Berlin with a highway-canal-railroad blockade. The Western allies defeated the blockade by supplying West Berlin with a gigantic airlift.

Critical situations developed in other parts of the globe. In the Far East, Chiang Kai-shek and the Chinese Nationalists were driven off China's mainland and fled to Formosa.

In Indo-China, the Communists gained half of Vietnam in a rebellion against the French colonial government. Britain and France refused an American invitation to join in armed intervention.

Trouble flared in the Middle East when President Nasser of Egypt seized the Suez Canal in July, 1956. Only America's persuasion called a halt to military action by Britain and France.

A Middle Eastern tier of nations signed the Baghdad Pact—alliance for mutual defense. The United States endorsed the pact's goal of repelling aggressions.

The Korean War began on June 25, 1950, when the North Korean Commu-

nists, without warning, crossed the Thirty-eighth Parallel dividing line and invaded South Korea. The United Nations declared North Korea an aggressor, and President Truman ordered American armed forces to South Korea's defense.

General Douglas A. MacArthur was appointed as Supreme Commander of U.N. forces in Korea. American naval units rushed to Korean waters and planes and troops were sent from the occupation forces in Japan.

The North Koreans were armed with Russian-made weapons and the South Koreans were unprepared for the attack. The Communists quickly drove the U.N. —South Korean defenders into the southeastern tip of Korea. MacArthur forces made a surprise landing at Inchon, on the western coast of Korea, and the war became a see-saw battle. The U.N. forced the North Koreans back across the Thirty-eighth Parallel and battered on toward the Yalu River border between China and Korea. On October 26, 1950, the Chinese Communists invaded from Manchuria and joined the North Koreans.

Once again the tide of battle turned and MacArthur's army was forced back across the Thirty-eighth. MacArthur had orders to avoid spreading the war into China, but he threatened to bomb Chinese bases to relieve the pressure on his army.

President Truman relieved MacArthur of command, saying the general had exceeded his authority and violated U.N. policy. General Matthew B. Ridgway was given command and the U.N. again fought its way North.

The Korean War ended in a stalemate. After two years of negotiations, a truce was signed on July 26, 1953. The Thirty-eighth Parallel again became Korea's dividing line.

General Dwight D. Eisenhower, the World War II leader, had become America's popular President. Eisenhower was elected in 1952 and reelected in 1956— each time with a tremendous popular vote.

Eisenhower proposed an Atoms for Peace plan which was adopted by eighty-two nations. Included was the Soviet Union, which had not agreed on any plan for control of atomic weapons.

Here at home, the United States faced inflation as postwar wages and prices spiraled. The nation's two great labor organizations merged as the AFL-CIO. And America's scientists were extremely busy . . . outer space was beckoning!

THE ERA OF ROCKET PROPULSION—

After World War II, the major powers concentrated on development of a new and mighty force, rocket propulsion. Experiments in guided missiles were stressed.

The American army used the first rocket gun, the "Bazooka," against axis foes. The Germans hit London with V-2 rockets. America's navy fired guided missiles in Korea. The possibilities of rocket propulsion spurred scientists' ambitions to penetrate outer space.

In the Cold War conflict between democracy and communism, the free world looked to President Eisenhower for leadership in preserving peace. Nikita Khrushchev was the Soviet Union's new leader.

Many trouble spots existed in the uneasy world. In the Middle East, President Nasser of Egypt became the "strong man" of the Arab world after his seizure of the Suez Canal. In April, 1957, Nasser reopened the Canal as his power rose.

OPENED THE DOOR TO OUTER SPACE

Newly-emancipated African nations met difficulties in change-over to native rule after long control by Europeans. Numerous disorders caused concern in United Nations.

In the Far East, the conflict grew between the Chinese Communists and Chiang Kai-shek's Nationalists. The Reds shelled the offshore islands of Quemoy and Matsu, held by Nationalists, creating problem for the United States.

The U.N. General Assembly, with all members voting, pushed for peace measures. The Soviet Union often used Security Council veto.

Fidel Castro gained attention by leading a rebellion in Cuba against President Fulgencio Batista. Although defeated in early efforts, Castro led his revolt from mountain hideouts and many followers joined his cause.

REGISTER
IT IS YOUR RIGHT!

VOTING R

A NEW CIVIL RIGHTS ACT, passed on September 9, 1957, provided added guarantees of political equality. The measure, first of its kind since 1875, created a bipartisan commission on civil rights. The commission's duty was to insure the equal rights of all to voting privileges and protection of the laws, regardless of race, color, national origin or religion. The commission was given the power to subpoena defendants and witnesses and conduct hearings in instances where the violation of civil rights was charged.

The new act authorized the Civil Rights Commission to seek federal district court injunctions against interference with voting rights. Civil contempt proceedings could be brought when the commission's orders were not complied with. Jury trials were not required when the maximum fine involved was no more than $300 and the jail sentence did not exceed forty-five days. Defendants could demand jury trials if the penalties were greater. A Reconstruction period law of 1866, which had empowered the President of the United States to enforce civil rights through the use of troops, if necessary, was repealed by the new act.

Eisenhower, in asking Congress to establish the Civil Rights Commission, wanted a stronger measure. The bill, as passed, was a modified version of his request. Eisenhower supported the civil rights program, which had gained strength during the Truman administration. In November, 1957, the President appointed retired Supreme Court Justice Stanley F. Reed as chairman of the Civil Rights Commission. Doctor John A. Hannah, president of Michigan State University, was named vice-chairman.

THE SCHOOL INTEGRATION issue reached its first major challenge at Little Rock, Arkansas, in September, 1957. The desegregation of all public schools had been ordered by the Supreme Court two years earlier. With the 1957 fall term nearing, the Little Rock school board obtained federal approval of a plan for gradual integration. The first Negroes were to be admitted to the formerly all-white Central High School. A state court issued an injunction against the integration, but that order was nullified by a federal district judge on August 30.

The day before school opened on September 2, Governor Orval M. Faubus of Arkansas called out the national guard "to prevent disorder." Nine Negro students were prevented from entering the school on September 4 when national guardsmen and state police surrounded the building. Five days later, white youths and adults turned back six Negro students attempting to enter a suburban all-white high school in North Little Rock. At Faubus' request the governor met with President Eisenhower on September 14. After the meeting, Governor Faubus said that the Supreme Court "is the law of the land and must be obeyed."

The National Guard was not withdrawn, however, until a federal injunction was issued against further interference. Rioting broke out when school officials admitted nine Negro students to Central High on September 23. The Negroes were sent home. The President then ordered 1,000 United States paratroopers to Little Rock and placed the state guard under federal command. On September 25, the Negroes were escorted into the school and guarded on leaving by United States troops armed with rifles and bayonets. School integration was thus brought about at Little Rock and the federal troops were gradually withdrawn.

A "man-made moon" was hurled into orbit around the earth by Russia, and the race for space began! On October 4, 1957, the Soviets made a stunning announcement—they had put the first artificial satellite into orbit. They called it Sputnik I. The world was surprised and excited. For days, Sputnik I was eagerly clocked as it hurtled in elliptical (egg-shaped) orbits around the earth every hour and a half. The "beep-beep" of its radio signal was heard until it fell silent on October 26. Sputnik I whirled on until its 18,000-mile-an-hour speed diminished. The satellite then returned to the earth's denser atmosphere and disintegrated.

Sputnik I was an aluminum sphere twenty-two inches in diameter and weighing 184 pounds. The satellite was carried into space in the nose cone of a towering rocket. A series of three engines propelled the rocket. The first stage engine lifted the rocket off the ground and thrust it into the skies at 4,500 miles an hour. After burning up its fuel, the first engine fell away. Stage two fired and boosted the speed to 12,000 miles an hour. By now, the rocket's path had curved and was circling the earth.

Stage three engine gave the final thrust. At this point, the rocket and nose cone fell away, and the satellite was launched. In its orbits, Sputnik I's farthest distance from earth was 583 miles and its nearest 143. On November 3, the Russians launched Sputnik II which weighed 1,120 pounds. This second satellite carried a little female dog, Laika. Sputnik II's signals ceased on November 10, and dog lovers mourned for lost Laika —but Russia's advancement in space science was dramatically demonstrated.

A NEW AGE OF SCIENCE began as the International Geophysical Year opened on July 1, 1957, An eighteen-month period was designated in which all nations were invited to participate in scientific research and experiments. A program was launched for advanced study of the earth, the seas, the atmosphere, the sun and outer space. Congress gave the National Science Foundation a $35,000,000 grant to underwrite America's participation.

AN AMERICAN SATELLITE was put into orbit less than four months after the Soviet feat. The United States was jubilant. Americans were chagrined when Russia was first with Sputniks I and II, but President Eisenhower assured them this country was making progress in its own space program. The promise was fulfilled on January 31, 1958, when the army sent Explorer I circling around the earth. Explorer I outreached the Sputniks in distance. Its apogee (farthest point from earth) was 1,575 miles, compared to Sputnik II's 1,056. Its perigee (closest distance) was 219 miles, against Sputnik I's 143. Explorer I, weighing thirty pounds, was carried by a Jupiter-C rocket and was expected to continue orbiting around the earth for several years to come.

A second space triumph for America was the navy's orbiting of Vanguard I on March 17, 1958. This outer space mite weighing only three and one-quarter pounds, reached an apogee of 2,513 miles. Vanguard I settled into a "life expectancy" of from two centuries to 1,000 years of whirling through space. The United States scored further satellite successes during 1958. On March 26, Explorer III was sent to join Explorer I and Vanguard I. On October 11, an Air Force Pioneer rocket was launched in an effort to orbit the moon. Although failing in that mission, the Pioneer penetrated space to a distance of 79,173 miles.

The military possibilities of rockets of great range developed with the space experiments. On November 28, an Atlas intercontinental ballistic missile (ICBM) was successfully test-fired, striking its oceanic target area 6,325 miles away. The possibilities of space explora-

tion also were developed. On May 15, the Russians orbited Sputnik III, weighing 2,925 pounds. On December 18, an 8,700-pound Atlas satellite was put in orbit by the United States. Space "vehicles" were becoming larger, large enough to carry a man, instead of a little dog.

A HOSTILE RECEPTION was given Vice-President Nixon on a tour of South America. Mobs attempted to attack the Vice-President and Mrs. Nixon at Lima, Peru, and Caracas, Venezuela. The government of both republics said the demonstrations were Communist-inspired. Nixon left Washington on April 27, 1958, to tour Argentina, Uruguay, Paraguay, Bolivia, Peru, Ecuador, Colombia and Venezuela. The first indication of hostility came on the opening visit, at Montevideo, Uruguay. A group of students crowded around the Vice-President's car, shouting, "Get out, Nixon!" Otherwise, Uruguay's welcome was warm.

In Buenos Aires, Nixon attended the inauguration of Arturo Frondizi, first constitutional president of Argentina in twelve years. The Vice-President said in his address, "Dictatorships are repugnant to our people." The Nixon party was cordially received on the next visits to Paraguay and Bolivia. But at Lima, on May 7, a Communist-led crowd of 1,000 stormed outside Nixon's hotel, clamoring, "Out with Nixon!" A mob of 2,000 students jeered the Vice-President as he attempted to speak at San Marcos University the next day. The Nixon party was pelted with stones and eggs. One rock grazed the Vice-President's neck.

Friendly visits followed at Ecuador and Colombia, but the anti-American demonstration in Venezuela was the most violent of the tour. Despite warnings of a reported plot to assassinate him, Nixon insisted on visiting Caracas. A mob of 200 broke the windows of the cars in which Nixon and Mrs. Nixon were riding. Secret service men drew their pistols as the mob attempted to drag the Vice-President and his wife from their cars. Nixon remained in the United States embassy until he decided to cut his visit short and fly to Puerto Rico. On his return to Washington, the Vice-President was given a hero's welcome. Nixon said that the United States should give "top priority" to its Latin American relations.

AMERICAN TROOPS LANDED in Lebanon as rebellion flared in the Middle East. The Eisenhower Doctrine was applied when a series of conflicts led to a general crisis. Following his seizure of the Suez Canal in 1956, President Nasser of Egypt had become the most powerful figure in the Arab world. A United Arab Republic (U.A.R.) was formed in February, 1958, by Egypt and Syria with Nasser as president. Neighboring states protested to the United Nations that pro-Nasser revolutionists were attempting to gain control of their governments. An armed revolution broke out in Lebanon on May 9, 1958, and Prime Minister Charles Malik asked the U.N. to intervene.

Observers sent to Lebanon by the U.N. Security Council reported that there was little evidence of Nasser support of the rebels. Nevertheless, fighting continued and President Eisenhower ordered the Sixth Fleet to eastern Mediterranean waters. On July 14, 1958, King Feisal II and Crown Prince Abdul Illad of Iraq were murdered in a pre-dawn raid on their palace. Officers of the Iraqi army seized the government. The next day, July 15, United States Marines landed in Lebanon. Eisenhower told Congress in a special message that he had ordered the occupation at the urgent request of President Camille Chamoun of Lebanon.

A similar revolt in Jordan threatened King Hussein's rule and the monarch asked Britain's protection. Two thousand British paratroopers were flown into Jordan. The American and British troops remained on guard duty in Lebanon and Jordan for several weeks. Dag Hammarskjold, Secretary-General of the U.N., visited the Middle East and reported that the dangers of revolution in Lebanon and Jordan had subsided. Late in September, the American and British troops were withdrawn from these areas.

TWO AMERICAN ATOMIC submarines crossed the North Pole under the Arctic icecap in August, 1958. The nuclear-powered *Nautilus* made the first undersea polar crossing on August 3. Under the direction of Commander William Robert Anderson, the *Nautilus* made the crossing during a record-breaking trip from Honolulu to Iceland. The *Nautilus* cruised submerged from Honolulu to the Bering Strait — 2,901 miles — averaging twenty knots. The submarine surfaced briefly near Point Barrow, Alaska, then submerged and headed for the North Pole.

The Nautilus nosed ahead under ice averaging twelve feet in thickness but extending downward to fifty feet in some places. After crossing the Pole, the submarine continued into the Atlantic Ocean and surfaced again between Spitzbergen and Greenland. The craft had cruised for ninety-six hours under ice and arctic waters. All who participated in the *Nautilus'* cruise were awarded a Presidential Citation, which said the *Nautilus* had uncovered a sub-polar route for future atomic cargo submarines.

The second atomic submarine to cross the North Pole underwater was the *Skate*, commanded by Commander James F. Calvert. The *Skate* duplicated the *Nautilus'* feat on August 11, traveling from New London, Connecticut. Another record was established by the *Seawolf*, which surfaced on October 6, 1958, after remaining submerged for sixty days. In August, 1962, two of the atomic submarines rendezvoused under ice at the North Pole. The United States developed a major nuclear-powered submarine program. Some of the submarines were armed with Polaris rocket missiles. The Polaris, carrying nuclear warheads, could be launched underwater and had a range of more than 1,500 miles. Rear Admiral Hyman G. Rickover pioneered the atomic submarine program, for which he was awarded a special gold medal by Congress.

THE CHINESE COMMUNISTS resumed their bombardment of the offshore islands of Quemoy and Matsu in August, 1958. A new crisis arose in this tense Far Eastern situation. The United States was in a delicate position in regard to the islands, which were held by Chiang Kai-shek's Nationalist troops. In January, 1955, Congress had adopted the Formosa Resolution, giving the President power to defend Formosa, the Pescadores and "related positions." Whether that included Quemoy and Matsu was left unstated.

When the Communists renewed shelling the islands from the mainland, Eisenhower ordered the Seventh Fleet to the Strait of Formosa. American warships, including aircraft carriers, began escorting Nationalist convoys to the islands. The American vessels stopped three miles short, however, to avoid entering China's territorial waters. The Communist artillery laid a curtain of shells around the islands and the Nationalist supply ships had difficulty getting through to docks. President Eisenhower declared that Quemoy and Matsu were becoming "increasingly related to the defense of Formosa." Some people took this as a commitment to defend them.

Talks on the Formosa situation were held at Warsaw by the United States and Red China through their ambassadors to Poland. After a brief "cease-fire" on October 6, Red China announced a new decision—the Communists reserved the right to shell Quemoy and Matsu on alternate days of each month. Secretary of State John Foster Dulles flew to Formosa for talks with Chiang Kai-shek. Following the meeting, the Nationalist leader announced he would not attempt to reconquer the Red Chinese mainland. The crisis was eased for the moment.

EDUCATION FOR DEFENSE! Congress planned a program of helping Young America become better prepared to cope with world problems of the future. In September, 1958, the National Defense Education Act was adopted. It provided federal funds to enable both schools and students to broaden their programs. A fund of $295,000,000 was voted for loans of up to $1,000 a year for a four year period repayable over ten years. Fifty per cent of the debt was forgiven if the student borrower, after graduation, taught for a period of five years in the nation's elementary or secondary schools.

Sciences and modern foreign languages were encouraged by a second appropriation of $280,000,000. With matching state funds, schools which qualified were offered assistance in building laboratories and installing equipment for science study. Also included were special facilities for study of the foreign languages which fit into America's international picture. A sum of $28,000,000 was earmarked for language study in colleges and universities. The act made 5,500 fellowships available for graduate students preparing to teach in higher institutions.

Such educational aids as radio, television and motion pictures were included in the program. The National Defense Education Act provided for funds to help schools install facilities for these media. The new program placed much stress on the sciences. Many schools which previously had not possessed adequate facilities for full science courses quickly obtained them. On qualifying and receiving the federal rating and assistance under the act, participating colleges became known as "national defense" schools.

Geophysical Year Expanded Man's Knowledge

Thousands of amateur observers joined the professional scientists in tracking the first satellites circling the earth. Many radio amateurs picked up satellite signals.

A rocket fired by the Naval Research Laboratory on San Nicolas Island, California, provided information on effects of the sun's radiation on communications in space.

MANY SCIENTIFIC DISCOVERIES were made during the International Geophysical Year, which began on July 1, 1957, and ended on December 31, 1958. More than seventy nations participated in this gigantic study of the planet Earth and its relationship to the universe. Thousands of scientists and technicians conducted research. Government and private scientific organizations operated more than 2,500 major stations. The Geophysical Year embraced observations and research in all physical and atmospheric sciences. Data and measurements were assembled which would require many years for complete study and analysis.

The first artificial earth satellites were launched and thousands of amateur and volunteer trackers followed their courses. Valuable data on weather and radio communications contributed new techniques and opened new fields in these sciences. Soundings were made in the world's oceans and greater depths discovered. Major explorations and research produced much information about Antarctica. The Geophysical Year was extended through 1959 as man gained vast new knowledge about the planet on which he lives and the universe surrounding it.

Sir Edmund Hillary's expedition in 1957-1958 confirmed that Antarctica is a single large continent. Americans discovered a mountain range.

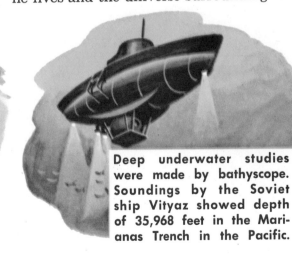

Deep underwater studies were made by bathyscope. Soundings by the Soviet ship Vityaz showed depth of 35,968 feet in the Marianas Trench in the Pacific.

FIDEL CASTRO SEIZED POWER in Cuba after more than five years of revolution against Fulgencio Batista's rule. Castro's final conquest of Cuba came on January 2, 1959, when his rebel army stormed into Havana. It climaxed the "26th of July Movement" which Castro launched on that day in 1953. In this first venture, Castro led 165 youthful rebels against the army barracks at Santiago de Cuba. Half of his men were killed and Castro and his younger brother, Raul, were thrown in prison.

Freed in 1955, Castro made new revolutionary plans while in the United States and Mexico. On December 2, 1956, he landed with fewer than one hundred men in Oriente Province of Cuba. Batista's soldiers killed most of the invaders and Castro fled to the mountains. The revolution appeared doomed, but soon began to gather strength as Cubans flocked to Castro's colors. From his mountain headquarters, Castro directed constant guerrilla warfare that harassed the Batista forces for two years.

Castro abandoned his guerrilla tactics and began a full-scale drive toward Havana from Oriente Province. His army grew as thousands of other Cubans, who regarded Batista as a tyrant, joined along the way. As the rebels advanced, Batista resigned as Cuba's president on January 1, 1959, and fled with his family to the Dominican Republic. Castro's troops entered Havana on January 2 and the jubilant leader followed in triumph six days later. Castro proclaimed a provisional Cuban government with Manuel Urrutia, a former Santiago de Cuba judge, as president. The United States recognized the new government on January 7. Castro, who became premier, promised free elections at the end of eighteen months. Many regarded him as a hero.

THE ST. LAWRENCE SEAWAY, opening the Great Lakes to large ocean steamships, was dedicated on June 26-27, 1959. The St. Lawrence Seaway, costing $500,-000,000, was the largest waterway project since the Panama Canal. The Wiley-Dondero Act of 1954 created the St. Lawrence Seaway Development Corporation and authorized the necessary work in United States territory. Working together, the United States and Canada constructed the St. Lawrence Seaway as the middle link in the vast overall St. Lawrence Waterway from the

Atlantic Ocean to the Great Lakes.

The seaway provided a 400-mile navigable route connecting the St. Lawrence River with the Great Lakes. It accommodated ocean-going ships of twenty-seven foot draft. The seaway completed a 2,342-mile deep water route from the Atlantic to Duluth, Minnesota, on Lake Superior. It made possible the development of the great international inland Port of Chicago. The seaway was opened to commerce on April 25, 1959, when

Canadian icebreaker *d'Iberville* passed through St. Lambert Lock near Montreal.

Queen Elizabeth II came from England to join President Eisenhower in the formal dedication of the seaway on June 26 at the St. Lambert Lock. The queen said the seaway was "one of the outstanding engineering accomplishments of modern times." The President hailed it as "a magnificent symbol to the entire world of the achievements possible to democratic nations peacefully working together for the common good." Queen Elizabeth the next day joined Vice-President Nixon at Massena, New York, for the dedication of the $650,000,000 St. Lawrence hydroelectric project. Before returning to England, Queen Elizabeth and Prince Philip paid a thirteen-hour visit to Chicago and toured the city. It was the first visit to Chicago by a reigning sovereign of Great Britain in the history of that nation.

ALASKA AND HAWAII were admitted to the Union in 1959—the first new states since Arizona's admission in 1912. Much enthusiasm had developed in the United States for the granting of statehood to the two colorful territories. On January 3, 1959, President Eisenhower signed the legislation admitting Alaska as the forty-ninth state. Two Democratic senators elected by the Alaska citizens, E. L. Bartlett and Ernest Gruening, took their seats in Congress. The President also signed an executive order redesigning the flag with seven rows of seven stars. The new design did not last long—On March 18, Eisenhower signed the bill admitting Hawaii as the fiftieth state. The President said that he did so "with great satisfaction." The Hawaiian people, with equal satisfaction, proceeded with the formalities of admission to the Union. Again the flag was rearranged—this time with five rows of six stars and four rows of five.

Voters of the islands on June 27 approved by nearly twenty to one their admission as a state. On July 28, they elected their first federal and state officials. William F. Quinn, Eisenhower's appointee as territorial governor since 1957, became Hawaii's first elected governor. Two United States senators of Oriental ancestry were elected—Hiram Leong Fong, a Republican, and Daniel K. Inouye, a Democrat. Fong was a Chinese-American businessman and Inouye a Japanese-American war veteran. President Eisenhower hailed their elections as "a very fine example of democracy at work, in operation, and I believe it is a good example for the whole world." In White House ceremonies on August 21, the President officially proclaimed Hawaii as the fiftieth state. An American dream in far-flung lands had finally come true.

KHRUSHCHEV VISITED AMERICA and spent thirteen days viewing the way of life in this country. During the trip, the Soviet premier met with the press and the Senate Foreign Relations Committee. He visited California and farms in Iowa. He talked with the people, from celebrities to laborers. Khrushchev closed his visit with a three-day conference with President Eisenhower—after which the prospects for a peaceful settlement in Berlin appeared very much brighter.

Khrushchev arrived in Washington on September 15, 1959, and made a helicopter tour of the capital with the President. In an address before the National Press Club at Washington, Khrushchev offered an explanation of what he had meant when he said, "We will bury you." It was a figure of speech, Khrushchev said, merely expressing his confidence that Communism would prevail over capitalism. The Soviet premier made a tour of the nation escorted by Henry Cabot Lodge, United States ambassador to the U.N. Stops included New York, Los Angeles, San Francisco and Des Moines. At most places visited, Khrushchev was given courteous but restrained receptions.

Eisenhower and Khrushchev conferred on September 25-27 at the President's Camp David retreat in Maryland. They issued a joint statement after the meeting, saying that Berlin negotiations would be "reopened with a view to achieving a solution which would be in accordance with the views of all concerned and in the interest of the maintenance of peace." Eisenhower said his talks with Khrushchev increased the probability of a summit meeting. The President also planned to visit the Soviet Union in 1960.

THREE MOON ROCKETS were successfully launched by the Soviets in 1959, giving them the lead in the race for outer space. The first rocket, called Lunik I, passed the moon and went into orbit around the sun—the first man-made planet to be put into the solar system. Lunik II hit the moon, and Lunik III circled the satellite and photographed its hidden side. All three were multi-stage rockets whose engines thrust them through space at 25,000 miles an hour.

Lunik I, launched on January 2, passed within 4,600 miles of the moon on January 4. The multiple firing stages were required to give the rocket sufficient speed to escape from the earth's gravity. The 3,245-pound vehicle carried radio transmitters which sent back data on radiation and other cosmic conditions. After passing the moon, Lunik I sped on into orbit around the sun on January 7. Lunik II, launched on September 12, hit the moon thirty-five hours and 236,875 miles later. An 860-pound instrument container was flung from the rocket near the moon, and this was the missile that struck. The impact was recorded when the container's instruments ceased operating. The "moon strike" was confirmed by British scientists. The Soviets said that their latest missile planted pennants of the Soviet Union on the moon.

The Soviets launched Lunik III on October 4 and this rocket went in a figure-of-eight orbit around the earth and moon. It carried a 614-pound, top-shaped instrument container. On a signal from earth, a cover opened on the side of the container and two cameras took pictures. On October 27, Moscow released a picture showing hazy spots which the Russians described as mountains and craters on the moon's surface. President Eisenhower joined other world leaders in congratulating the Soviet government for its scientific achievements. On March 3, 1959, the United States also had sent a rocket—Pioneer IV—into orbit around the sun, but Congress was dissatisfied. Greater efforts were ordered to overtake the Soviets in space—regardless of cost.

PRESIDENT EISENHOWER VISITED

eleven nations on three continents in a widely hailed peace mission. The President traveled 22,000 miles in nineteen days. A three-day Western Summit Conference in Paris concluded the tour. Before his departure from Washington on December 3, 1959, Eisenhower said, "During this mission of peace and good will, I hope to promote a better understanding of America and to learn more of our friends abroad." On his visits to capitals in Europe, Asia and Africa, the President was cheered by several millions of the nations' peoples who greeted him. Everywhere, he met warm welcomes.

Eisenhower's journey carried him to Italy, Turkey, Pakistan, Afghanistan, India, Iran, Greece, Tunisia, France, Spain and Morocco. The President received an ovation in Turkey which he called "the most stupendous I have ever seen." An estimated 1,000,000 spectators lined the streets of New Delhi to greet the President in India. Banners strung over streets proclaimed: "Eisenhower— Prince of Peace." Visiting India's World Agricultural Fair, Eisenhower said in an opening address, "There must be a world-wide war against hunger."

In Spain, the President visited the Torrejon Air Base near Madrid. He was greeted by Generalissimo Francisco Franco at the base, which was built by the United States. Eisenhower was accompanied on his tour by an official party of twenty-one members. Included was Under Secretary of State Robert Murphy, who headed the diplomatic advisors on the mission. The Western Summit talks began at Paris on December 19, at the conclusion of the goodwill visits.

Eisenhower conferred at Paris with Prime Minister Harold Macmillan of Great Britain, President Charles De Gaulle of France, and Chancellor Konrad Adenauer of West Germany. In private talks with De Gaulle, Eisenhower failed to weaken De Gaulle's opposition to the integration of French troops in NATO forces. The Western Summit talks reaffirmed the four governments' determination to stand together. Khrushchev was invited to join with Eisenhower, Macmillan and De Gaulle in East-West Summit discussions in Paris. The talks later were scheduled for May 16, 1960.

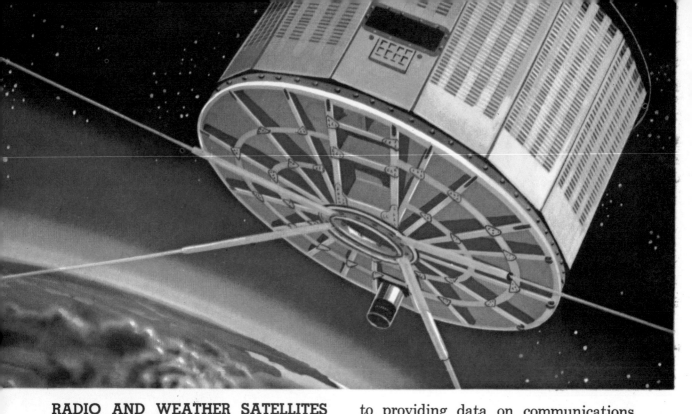

RADIO AND WEATHER SATELLITES

RADIO AND WEATHER SATELLITES launched by the United States added to man's growing knowledge of outer space. They demonstrated that radio communications could extend over millions of miles—and weather observations could be made from space. On March 11, 1960, the National Aeronautics and Space Administration launched Pioneer V at Cape Canaveral, Florida. The rocket was put into orbit around the sun as America's second man-made planet. The ninety-five pound sphere contained radio instruments, including two transmitters. The batteries were recharged by solar cells carried in four paddle wheels attached to the sphere's exterior.

The goal was to prove that radio contact could be maintained with a planetoid for 50,000,000 miles. Pioneer V transmitted until June 26, when the Jodrell Bank Radio Telescope station near Manchester, England, reported the last contact. At that point Pioneer V was 22,500,000 miles from earth. In addition to providing data on communications, Pioneer V measured radiation, magnetic fields and the density of cosmic dust. The information obtained indicated that space travelers of the future would require maximum protection from these.

Tiros I, the weather observer, was launched as an earth satellite on April 1—also at Cape Canaveral. This 270-pound hatbox-shaped missile carried television equipment, including two cameras. The camera with the larger lens had a photographic range of 64,000 square miles. The mission was to photograph weather phenomena in space and relay the pictures to earth. Seven hours after its launching, Tiros I sent four pictures of cloud covers over the Gulf of St. Lawrence. The curvature of the earth was plainly visible. Spiral patterns in some of the cloud formations were noted, indicating air streams. Meteorologists agreed that weather forecasting would be greatly aided by satellite observations to provide earlier tornado and hurricane warnings.

AN AMERICAN U-2 SPY PLANE was brought down 1,200 miles inside the Soviet Union—with explosive diplomatic consequences. The plane, piloted by Francis Gary Powers, was downed on May 1, 1960, while engaged in photographic reconnaissance. Relations between the United States and the Soviet Union became critical in a controversy over America's aerial intelligence activities. As a direct result, the Summit Conference scheduled at Paris on May 16 was canceled and Eisenhower's visit to Moscow, planned for September, was called off.

The first indication of the U-2 episode came on May 3 with a Washington report that an American weather plane was missing. On May 5, Premier Khrushchev told the Supreme Soviet that the American plane had been shot down inside Russia. He called it an "aggressive provocation aimed at wrecking the Summit Conference." Two days later, Khru-

shchev said that Powers, the pilot, was alive and had confessed to the spy mission. The Soviet premier said that the U-2 (a high-altitude Lockheed) had been hit by a rocket while flying at 65,000 feet. On May 10, Khrushchev threatened to use rockets against any nation permitting American planes to use bases in their territories for spy flights. The State Department said the United States would defend its allies if Russia attacked them.

President Eisenhower assumed the full responsibility for the U-2 flights, which had been in operation for nearly four years. In a statement on May 11, the President said, "Intelligence activity is a distasteful necessity . . . but no one wants another Pearl Harbor. This means that we must have knowledge of military forces and preparations around the world. Secrecy in the Soviet Union makes this essential." The Soviet government made a stern formal protest to Washington.

THE SUMMIT CONFERENCE was torpedoed as the scene of the U-2 crisis shifted to Paris. Arriving on May 14, Khrushchev aroused hopes when he pledged to "exert all effort to make the conference a success." The next day, however, the Soviet premier issued an ultimatum through the British and French governments. He demanded that the United States end flights over Russia, apologize for past "aggressions," and punish those who were responsible for ordering the U-2 flights. Otherwise, Khrushchev declared, there would be no Summit Conference. President Eisenhower, informed of Soviet demands, said the flights had been stopped —but there would be no apology.

A premilinary meeting was held on May 16 by heads of the four governments to discuss whether the Summit talks would be held. Khrushchev bitterly denounced the United States and repeated his demands. Again, Eisenhower refused to apologize or punish those connected with past U-2 flights. Khrushchev withdrew the Soviet government's invitation for Eisenhower's visit. De Gaulle and Macmillan urged Khrushchev not to release his speech for publication. They pleaded with him not to wreck the Summit talks—but Khrushchev refused and stalked angrily out of the meeting.

The death blow to the conference came the next day, May 17. De Gaulle invited Eisenhower, Macmillan and Khrushchev to meet with him and make one more effort to save the crucial talks. Eisenhower and Macmillan accepted, but Khrushchev refused to discuss the matter further unless his ultimatum was accepted. The Summit Conference was called off and America's relations with the Soviet Union became more strained.

Powers was convicted of espionage in his Moscow trial. Present at the trial were the U-2 pilot's parents, Mr. and Mrs. Oliver W. Powers, and his wife, Mrs. Barabara Powers. The American repeated his confession, saying he had flown the plane as a civilian pilot for the Central Intelligence Agency. Powers could not confirm that a rocket had shot him down. He said he had "heard and felt a hollow-sounding explosion" and saw "an orange-colored light." Powers said he parachuted to safety. On August 19, 1960, Powers was sentenced to ten years. After serving twenty-one months, he was freed in 1962 in an exchange for a Soviet spy held by the United States.

THE KENNEDY-NIXON TV DEBATES

prior to the 1960 election introduced a new technique of Presidential campaigning. Following their nominations, Senator John F. Kennedy and Vice-President Nixon appeared in four nationally televised one-hour debates. For the first time, millions of Americans saw and heard Presidential candidates in virtually face-to-face discussion. Kennedy had been nominated by the Democrats at Los Angeles, with Senator Lyndon B. Johnson of Texas named for Vice-President. The Republicans nominated Nixon at Chicago, with Henry Cabot Lodge as his running mate. The widely-known Nixon, against the counsel of many advisors, agreed to debate on TV with Kennedy.

In the first debate, televised from Chicago on September 26, Kennedy and Nixon disagreed on such domestic issues as farm support, minimum wages, and medical care for the aged. On the Soviet Union and Communist China, Kennedy said the only way the United States could "stay ahead" in the "deadly competition" was to "move ahead." Nixon said he and Kennedy were "not in disagreement as to the aims. The question is the means." Offshore Chinese islands of Quemoy and Matsu dominated the second debate held October 7 in Washington. Kennedy declared, "We have never said flatly that we will defend Quemoy and Matsu if attacked. We say we will defend them if it's part of a general attack on Formosa." Nixon disagreed, saying, "These islands are in the area of freedom. We should not force our Nationalist allies to get off of them and give them to the Communists."

Quemoy and Matsu were discussed again in the third debate, October 13, with Kennedy in New York and Nixon in Hollywood. The fourth debate, at New York on October 21, centered on the subject of Castro and Cuba. Nixon criticized as "dangerously irresponsible" Kennedy's idea of helping anti-Castro groups "within and without Cuba." Kennedy replied that Nixon's proposed "quarantine of Cuba" would be ineffective. At the conclusion of the debates, political observers said that Kennedy had emerged far better known to the American people than he had been before—and he had proved he was not an "immature" candidate.

Official returns of the voting on November 8, 1960, gave Kennedy a final margin over Nixon of 118,550 votes—the closest popular vote in a Presidential election since 1884. Kennedy's margin in the Electoral College was 303 votes to Nixon's 219—the closest since 1916. In some states where the returns were particularly close, such as Illinois and Texas, Republican leaders demanded recounts. There were charges of election frauds in some cases, resulting in lawsuits. Kennedy's election was assured when Illinois' twenty-seven electoral votes were certified to him on December 14. The 1960 election brought out the greatest popular vote in Presidential history. Nearly sixty-nine million ballots were cast. Of four minor party candidates, Governor Orval Faubus of Arkansas received the highest vote. Running on the National States' Rights ticket, Faubus polled 214,549 votes. Other minor party candidates and their votes were: Eric Hass, Socialist Labor, 46,560; Rutherford B. Decker, Prohibition, 46,203, and Farrell Dobbs, Socialist Workers, 39,541. The Democrats retained control of both the House of Representatives and the Senate, although the Republicans made slight gains.

JOHN F. KENNEDY WAS ELECTED President by a margin so narrow that some states conducted recounts. The election of Kennedy as the thirty-fifth President was not finally decided until the electoral vote count on December 19.

KENNEDY WAS THE YOUNGEST President to be elected to the office, forty-three years of age. Theodore Roosevelt was the youngest man to become President. As Vice-President, Roosevelt was forty-two when he took office following the assassination of William McKinley in 1901. That Kennedy's showing in the debates with Nixon had much to do with his election was conceded. Henry M. Jackson, Democratic National Chairman, said the "biggest single factor" was Nixon's agreement to participate in the debates. Kennedy himself did not think he would have won without the debates.

President Kennedy was born at Brookline, Massachusetts, on May 29, 1917. He was the son of Joseph P. Kennedy, banker, realtor and former ambassador to Great Britain. During his junior year at Harvard, Kennedy worked for six months in the London embassy while his father was ambassador. The new President was a 1940 graduate of Harvard with the degree of Bachelor of Science cum laude (with honors). Kennedy served in the navy during World War II, from 1941 to 1945. He was commander of PT Boat 109 in the Solomon Islands campaign and won the Navy and Marine Corps Medal.

Serving briefly as a news correspondent, Kennedy covered the Potsdam Conference shortly before the end of the war. He then entered politics and was elected to three terms as Democratic congressman from Massachusetts, the first time in 1947. Kennedy was elected to the Senate in a surprising victory in 1952 over Henry Cabot Lodge. The new First Lady was Mrs. Jacqueline Bouvier Kennedy. The Kennedys had a three-year-old daughter, Caroline. A son was born shortly after the election and was named John F. Jr. Kennedy was the first Roman Catholic ever to be elected to the Presidency of the United States of America.

28,000,000 Population Gain!

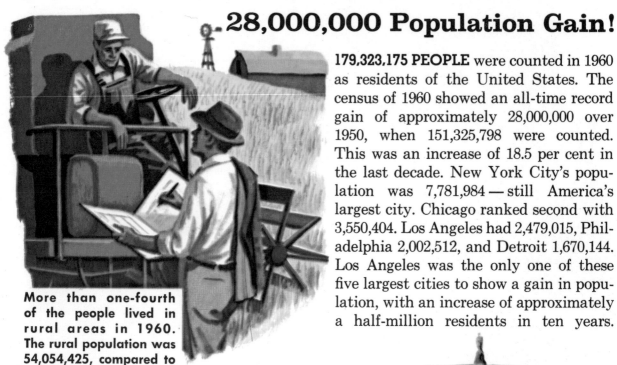

More than one-fourth of the people lived in rural areas in 1960. The rural population was 54,054,425, compared to 125,268,750 in cities.

179,323,175 PEOPLE were counted in 1960 as residents of the United States. The census of 1960 showed an all-time record gain of approximately 28,000,000 over 1950, when 151,325,798 were counted. This was an increase of 18.5 per cent in the last decade. New York City's population was 7,781,984 — still America's largest city. Chicago ranked second with 3,550,404. Los Angeles had 2,479,015, Philadelphia 2,002,512, and Detroit 1,670,144. Los Angeles was the only one of these five largest cities to show a gain in population, with an increase of approximately a half-million residents in ten years.

Florida had the greatest ten-year gain among the states—78.7 per cent. Florida's 1950 population of 2,771,305 increased to 4,951,560.

Shifts in population altered representation in Congress. Changes were made in twenty-five states. California gained eight new seats. Pennsylvania lost three.

THE UNITED STATES BROKE OFF diplomatic relations with Cuba on January 3, 1961. In announcing the break with Castro's government, President Eisenhower said, "There is a limit to what the United States in self-respect can endure. That limit has now been reached." A growing series of Castro abuses led to the severance of ties. Shortly after gaining power in Cuba in January, 1959, Castro began wholesale executions of former President Batista's supporters. Revolutionary courts tried hundreds on charges of torture and murder of anti-Batista Cubans. During the first four months of Castro's rule, more than 500 were executed by firing squads. The shootings were denounced on the United States Senate floor as a Cuban "blood bath."

Relations between the United States and Cuba steadily deteriorated. Early in his dictatorship, Castro established economic and military ties with the Soviet Union. American-owned oil refineries and other businesses in Cuba were seized by the Castro government. The United States retaliated by first reducing the quotas and then suspended the purchase of Cuban sugar in America. The next step was to place an embargo on exports to Cuba except certain foods and medicines.

Castro issued threats against America's continued occupation of the Guantanamo naval base. The White House announced that Guantanamo would be defended if attacked. Communist-led invasions of Guatemala and Nicaragua appeared imminent, and American naval units were sent to Central American waters to "shoot if necessary" to prevent such attacks. By now, thousands of anti-Castro refugees had fled from Cuba to Florida. On December 3, 1960, Eisenhower authorized $1,000,000 for relief and re-settlement of the refugees. Castro demanded that the United States embassy personnel in Havana be reduced to eleven. This, Eisenhower decided, was "the limit." The break with the now openly pro-Soviet Castro inevitably followed.

A "NEW FRONTIER" FOR AMERICA

was launched as President Kennedy took office on January 20, 1961. In his inaugural address, Kennedy called for a "grand and global alliance" to combat "the common enemies of man: tyranny, poverty, disease and war itself." He pledged support of the United Nations and America's loyalty to its allies. Kennedy announced readiness to resume negotiations with the Soviet Union, asking that "both sides begin anew the quest for peace." The President told the American people, "Let us never negotiate out of fear, but let us never fear to negotiate." Kennedy said, "In your hands, my fellow citizens, more than mine will rest the final success or failure of our course . . . And so, my fellow Americans, ask not what your country can do for you—ask what you can do for your country." The nation cheered.

A Peace Corps was established by Kennedy as the first step toward his New Frontier. On March 1, 1961, the President by executive order created the Peace Corps on a trial basis. He described the corps as "a pool of trained men and women sent overseas to help foreign countries meet their urgent needs for skilled manpower." Open to all qualified Americans, the corps sought men and women skilled in teaching, agriculture and health. None of the Peace Corps volunteers was paid a salary. The government paid for training, transportation, living expenses, medical care and administrative costs. The Peace Corps members lived at the same level as the peoples of the lands to which they were sent—doing the same work and eating the same food. The Peace Corps was permanently established by Congress in September, with $40,000,000 authorized for the first year. The President named R. Sargent Shriver, his brother-in-law, as the Corps' director.

A MAN IN SPACE! The Soviet Union won the race to space by putting a man into orbit around the earth. The coveted "first" was accomplished on April 12, 1961. Major Yuri Gagarin, a twenty-seven year old air force reserve pilot, was sent into orbit and made one circuit of the globe before landing safely. Gagarin's spacecraft was named the Vostok, meaning East. The vehicle, weighing five tons, was launched by a huge multi-stage rocket whose six engines gave it a thrust of 20,000,000 horsepower. The Vostok's flight required 108 minutes, eighty-nine of which were spent in orbit. Gagarin traveled at a top speed of 17,000 miles an hour. His distance from earth during the orbit varied from 108.76 to 187.66 miles. The Soviet's Gagarin experienced the "weightlessness" expected to be encountered by men venturing into space, and reported that he "withstood it well."

The Vostok was launched from a Soviet rocket base in Baikonur in southwest Siberia. Moscow's timetable of the flight logged the launching at 9:07 A.M.

on April 12. Fifteen minutes later—at 9:22—Gagarin radioed that he was passing over South America. At 10:15, he reported that he was over Africa. At 10:25, a signal from the ground fired the Vostok's braking rockets. The Soviets announced that Gagarin landed at 10:55 A.M. "in the prearranged area of the U.S.S.R.," 400 miles southeast of Moscow.

Gagarin was honored in a mammoth celebration at Moscow on April 14. Premier Khrushchev told the cosmonaut, "You are immortal because you are the first to penetrate into space." Gagarin was cited as Hero of the Soviet Union, the nation's highest honor. President Kennedy congratulated the Soviet Union on its scientific accomplishment, but discrepancies in Soviet accounts and Gagarin's own story aroused some doubts in America. However, Doctor Frank Press, a member of the President's science advisory committee, said, "There is no doubt that the Russians did what they said they did." America speeded efforts to regain ground in the space race.

AN ATTEMPTED INVASION of Cuba ended in disaster, and America's prestige suffered a blow. The United States was accused of planning the invasion and then failing to support it. Early in April, 1961, the Cuban National Revolutionary Council made an appeal in New York for all Cubans to join in an effort to overthrow Castro. Commenting on reports of an impending invasion, President Kennedy said every effort was being made to "make sure there are no Americans involved in any actions inside Cuba."

Three American-made B-26 bombers on April 15 raided Cuban bases near Havana, Santiago de Cuba, and San Antonio de los Banos. Seven Castro soldiers were killed and thirty-nine were wounded. Castro said the planes came from the United States as a "prelude to an invasion." On April 17, an invading force of 1,400—most of them Cuban exiles —sailed into Bahia de Cochinos (the Bay of Pigs). Supported by planes, the invaders landed on the beaches of Las Villas Province and advanced ten miles inland.

The invasion force was reported to have been recruited and equipped in the United States and trained in Guatemala.

Soviet Premier Khrushchev warned Kennedy that "we shall render the Cuban people and their government all necessary assistance in beating back the armed attack." The President replied that the United States planned no military intervention in Cuba, but neither would it permit any outside force to intervene. Meanwhile, the invasion collapsed as Castro forces launched a counterattack. Expected plane support failed to materialize and the invaders surrendered. Castro offered to exchange 1,167 prisoners for 500 American agricultural tractors. A Tractors for Freedom Committee was formed, and Kennedy urged Americans to contribute as private citizens— as the government could have no part in the negotiations. The prisoner exchange was delayed when Castro raised his price to a choice of 1,000 tractors, 500 bulldozers, or $28,000,000 cash. The invasion episode provoked criticism of America.

AMERICA'S FIRST SPACEMAN! An estimated 50,000,000 television viewers held their breaths as they watched a momentous countdown at Cape Canaveral on May 5, 1961. At 10:34 A.M. (eastern daylight time), a huge Redstone rocket blasted aloft carrying into space the American astronaut—Commander Alan B. Shepard, Jr., of the United States Navy. Shepard rode in a 4,040-pound Mercury capsule named Freedom 7. With relief and pride, the vast American television audience saw the rocket rise and then arch far off into the distance, leaving a comet-like trail as it disappeared.

Shepard's capsule carried him 116.5 miles into the air and reached a speed of 5,100 miles an hour. The sub-orbital flight lasted for fifteen minutes, the Freedom 7 landing in the Atlantic Ocean 302 miles from Cape Canaveral. A navy recovery task force was waiting and a Marine helicopter was only 700 feet away as a huge parachute brought the capsule to a safe landing in the sea. Both Shepard and the capsule were hoisted to the helicopter and delivered to the aircraft carrier *Lake Champlain*. President Kennedy, who had watched the launching on TV, telephoned to congratulate Shepard on the carrier.

Throughout the flight, Shepard sent a series of radio messages. Once he exclaimed, "What a beautiful view!" He reported that weightlessness at the top of the flight did not handicap him as he tested the capsule's manual controls. Shepard related how he released the retro-rockets to slow the capsule, and how he broke out the landing parachutes. Shepard's messages were relayed to radio and television as he sent them—adding to America's excitement and pride. Although Shepard and the Freedom 7 were not sent into orbit, the successful launching enabled the United States to regain ground in the space race with the Soviet Union. Yuri Gagarin, the Soviet cosmonaut, had orbited the earth in secrecy—Shepard's flight was announced beforehand and reported in full detail.

AMERICA REPEATED THE FEAT by putting a second astronaut into space on July 21, 1961. Captain Virgil I. (Gus) Grissom of the United States air force duplicated Shepard's sub-orbital flight. Grissom was rocketed aloft in a Mercury capsule named Liberty Bell 7—only slightly different from Freedom 7. Grissom was carried to an altitude of 118 miles at a top speed of 5,280 miles an hour. The capsule landed in the Atlantic 303 miles from Cape Canaveral and again a Marine helicopter was waiting.

While Grissom was making a check of his instrument readings, an escape hatch on the capsule blew off. The astronaut leaped into the water and swam for several minutes before being lifted to the helicopter. The capsule filled with water and sank, all films and other instrument records being lost. Both Shepard and Grissom withstood the strain of their space journeys without ill effects. President Kennedy also watched Grissom's flight on TV and telephoned his congratulations. America's first two "men in space" were awarded the Distinguished Service Medal of the National Aeronautical and Space Administration (NASA). The nation was much encouraged by its gains in the space race with the Russians.

SEVENTEEN ORBITS of the earth was the next Soviet space feat—accomplished by Major Gherman S. Titov. The second Soviet cosmonaut took off on an unannounced flight at 9 A.M. (Moscow time) on August 6, 1961. After Titov had circled the earth once in 88.6 minutes, the Soviet radio and TV revealed that the orbital marathon was in progress.

Titov was in flight for twenty-five hours and eighteen minutes. During his seventeen orbits, he passed over most of the world's inhabited areas. He radioed goodwill messages to the peoples of several nations as he passed overhead. At all times, Titov was from 110.3 to 115.3 miles above the earth. He traveled in a spacecraft named the Vostok II. Weighing 10,430 pounds, the vehicle was believed to be cylindrical in shape and about twenty feet long. It had a diameter of about fourteen feet. Titov had enough room for limited movements.

Television views of some of Titov's activities were released by Soviet space officials. The cosmonaut ate three meals of paste squeezed from tubes. He slept for several hours and twice maneuvered the spacecraft with manual controls. The Russians later said that Titov had been sent on his prolonged flight to determine the effects on man under those conditions. Titov said that weightlessness did not interfere with his handling of the ship. The cosmonaut landed in the Volga River region, 460 miles from Moscow, at 10:18 A.M. (Moscow time) on August 7. He traveled 437,500 miles in space, nearly the distance of a round trip to the moon.

Moscow hailed its new hero and the world applauded the cosmonaut's feat. Adlai E. Stevenson, United States ambassador to the U.N., extended this nation's congratulations to the Soviet government. He said, "This event sharpens the need for some international action to regulate the use of outer space for peaceful purposes and to keep the arms race from spreading to that field." American scientists agreed and applauded the Soviets' startling space capability.

A WALL DIVIDING BERLIN arose overnight to stop the mass flight of East Germans to West Germany. Since 1949, an estimated 2,000,000 East Germans had fled from the Communist-controlled area to West Germany. Shortly after midnight on August 13, 1961, the Communist governments suddenly ordered border controls established. Before dawn, the East Berlin authorities had constructed the first phases of a border wall dividing the city. The barrier denied East Berliners the right to cross into West Berlin without obtaining special permits.

More than 50,000 East Berliners awoke to find they could not cross to report for jobs which they held in West Berlin. Families were separated. The East German authorities said the wall was intended to control the movements of East Berliners only, but sixty-eight of eighty crossing points were closed. This soon was reduced to seven crossings and Western occupation forces were restricted to the use of only one crossing point. The United States, Britain and France protested that the pledge of free movement in Berlin and Germany was violated. Moscow replied that it was an internal matter involving East Germany alone.

The Soviets rejected every effort to remove the wall and restore free movement between East and West Berlin. The wall was extended until it consisted of a five-foot high stone barricade along nearly the entire twenty-five mile East-West border. President Kennedy ordered a 1,500-man battle group sent to reinforce the 5,000-man Berlin garrison. Numerous incidents of violence occurred at the wall. Some refugees seeking to escape into West Berlin were shot to death by East Berlin guards. In August, 1962, the Soviet leaders carried out their threat and abolished their East Berlin command. But the tension remained. Though retiring into East Germany, the Soviet Union retained control of East Berlin.

THE FIRST AMERICAN IN ORBIT was John H. Glenn, Marine Corps lieutenant colonel. Glenn circled the globe three times on February 20, 1962, to give the United States orbital status alongside the Russians. He rode a Mercury capsule named Friendship 7, which was hurled into orbit by an Atlas rocket launched at Cape Canaveral. Glenn's three orbits were made in four hours and fifty-six minutes. He landed in the Atlantic 700 miles southeast of Cape Canaveral, within six miles of the recovery destroyer Noa.

Glenn was acclaimed throughout America. He appeared before Congress and at the U.N. In New York City, an estimated 4,000,000 turned out to greet him. Glenn described in interviews some of his experiences while in orbit: "I saw three beautiful sunsets. The coast of Africa is a beautiful sight...I had a 900 mile view of the horizon. I looked back across Florida and saw the Mississippi delta...I had no ill effects of weightlessness. It was very pleasant." Glenn told of releasing his hold on a camera which he held in his hand. After operating a switch, he reached out and grasped the camera again—in midair! Glenn was taken to Grand Turk Island in the British Bahamas after being recovered from the sea. On Glenn's return to Cape Canaveral, President Kennedy met him there to extend a personal tribute on behalf of all America. Glenn's experience proved of great aid to all of the American astronauts who followed him into orbit.

Malcolm Scott Carpenter, a naval lieutenant commander, performed America's next orbital feat. On May 24, 1962, Carpenter also girdled the globe three times. He was launched in the capsule Aurora 7 from Cape Canaveral at 8:45 A.M. (eastern time). Twenty-five minutes later he was reported over Africa. Thirty minutes after that he was over Australia. This very speed at which Carpenter traveled gave America nationwide fright. Carpenter was five seconds late in firing his retro-rocket brakes—it caused him to overshoot the landing zone by 200 miles. For nearly an hour, America feared Carpenter was lost while the recovery fleet searched for him. The welcome news finally came—Carpenter had been sighted calmly sitting on a life raft!

A NEW ERA OF COMMUNICATIONS

was opened when the communications satellite Telstar was put into orbit around the earth. The Telstar, designed and built by the Bell Telephone system, was launched at Cape Canaveral on July 10, 1962. The project, thus privately developed and sponsored, was sent into space through cooperation with the NASA facilities at America's great launching base. The American Telephone and Telegraph Company paid the full cost of the launching, approximately $3,000,000, in addition to the many millions which the company invested in perfecting Telstar.

John R. Pierce of Bell Telephone laboratories proposed in 1954 that space satellites be used for communications. The telephone company undertook the project, with the purpose of providing a system for "live" overseas telecasts and unlimited facilities for telephone calls. Telstar was built at the Bell laboratories in New Jersey—the finished product being a spherical instrument container thirty-four and one-half inches in diameter. It had antennas powered by solar batteries for receiving and transmitting back to earth broadband microwave radio signals. With television waves moving in unbending lines from tower to tower, Telstar acted as a "tower-in-the-sky."

Shortly after Telstar went into orbit, the Bell company's satellite communication station in Maine began exchanging signals. Within a short time, the first telecasts relayed by Telstar were exchanged between the United States and Europe. The telecasts were "live," being picked up and re-transmitted by Telstar as swiftly as they were transmitted. The transmissions were made to Telstar as the satellite passed over designated positions. The re-telecast was beamed back and picked up by the receiving station on the other side of the ocean. President Kennedy sponsored a Telstar measure, authorizing the government to cooperate with private enterprises in further development of satellite communications.

ANTI-INTEGRATION RIOTS marked the enrollment of James H. Meredith as the first Negro student at the University of Mississippi. President Kennedy ordered troops to the college town of Oxford as United States marshals enforced a federal court order that Meredith be enrolled. Led by Governor Ross Barnett of Mississippi, bitter opposition was offered to desegregation at the state school. At the height of the disorders on September 30 and October 1, 1962, approximately 15,000 federal troops were massed in Oxford. Two men were killed, 75 were injured, and 112 of the rioters were arrested before the violence was suppressed.

Governor Barnett had ignored the court order to enroll Meredith, twenty-nine year old air force veteran. The decree was issued by a panel of eight federal judges at New Orleans. Meredith was denied admittance three times as he sought to enroll, once by the governor personally. On September 26, a force of 400 unarmed Mississippi highway patrolmen turned back Meredith and five cars of United States marshals. Additional marshals were rushed to Oxford and airborne troops were flown to the town. On September 30, President Kennedy ordered sufficient troops rushed to Oxford to enforce obedience to the court's decree.

General rioting broke out that night. The troops used tear gas and bayonets, but fired their guns over the rioters' heads, to quell the riots. Meanwhile, Governor Barnett bowed to the court and urged that peace be restored in Oxford. Meredith was enrolled on October 1 and was escorted by marshals as he attended his first classes. Governor Barnett was cited for contempt by the federal court. Former army Major General Edwin Walker had taken part in the incident by urging Mississippians to resist the troops—even offering to lead them. Walker appeared at the scene of the riots and was arrested on charges of "inciting to rebellion, insurrection and seditious conspiracy." Walker had commanded the troops sent to Little Rock to enforce school desegregation in 1957.

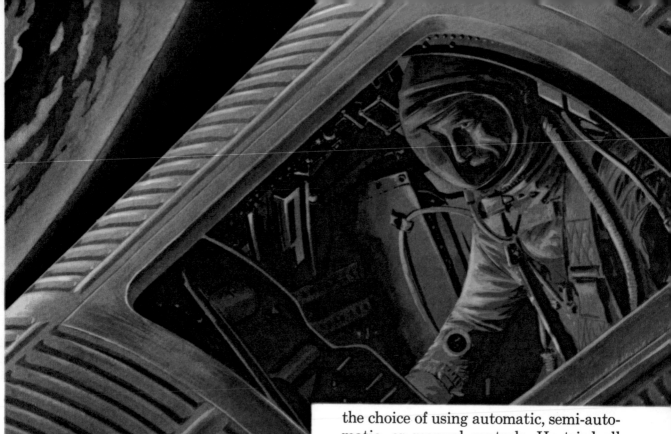

PRECISION IN SPACE TRAVEL was demonstrated by Walter M. Schirra, Jr., as he made America's third orbital flight. On October 3, 1962, Schirra, a navy commander, orbited the earth six times. Ending his 160,000 mile journey, he reached the Pacific Ocean recovery zone within two minutes of the estimated time. Schirra parachuted his capsule Sigma 7 into the ocean 9,000 yards from the prime recovery carrier *Kearsarge*. Jubilant NASA officials hailed Schirra's feat as a "space bullseye."

Schirra's six-orbit journey was, until then, America's most ambitious space venture. From the time Schirra and the Sigma 7 were lofted by an Atlas rocket at Cape Canaveral until they landed, nine hours and thirteen minutes elapsed. The astronaut and NASA officials described the flight as "perfect." Not a mishap or miscalculation developed. Schirra had the choice of using automatic, semi-automatic, or manual controls. He tried all three and reported flawless operation. Discussing the performance of Sigma 7, Schirra said, "What a sweet little bird!"

An air of confidence marked the new orbital triumph throughout. The astronaut himself held light-hearted conversations with his trackers. Schirra talked several times to America's two earlier orbital heroes—John H. Glenn, Jr., and M. Scott Carpenter. As he passed over Hawaii, Schirra said to the trackers there, "Aloha." When instructed by central control to continue his trip for six orbits, the astronaut exclaimed, "Hallelujah!" The smoothness of Schirra's flight encouraged America's space authorities. Walter Williams, Cape Canaveral project director, said a twenty-four hour, eighteen-orbit flight would be attempted early in 1963. Later in the year, two astronauts would be put in orbit in the same capsule. America had come far in the race to outer space.

CUBA WAS BLOCKADED by the United States to shut off the delivery of nuclear weapons by the Soviet Union. The two great powers came to a showdown over atomic missile bases built and armed in Cuba by the Soviets. America demanded that they be removed, and the world awaited the outcome during a week of crisis and anxiety. People everywhere had genuine fears that at any moment a deluge of long range missiles carrying warheads of atomic death might start falling on the earth.

America's distrust of Fidel Castro had built up toward the crisis. In September, 1962, Castro announced that a Cuban port was being outfitted to service the Soviet fishing fleet. This aroused suspicions that the fishing port actually might be a naval base. Then photographic reconnaissance by American planes detected the real menace—Soviet missile bases in Cuba! Launching pads had been installed and stocked with rockets capable of 1,200 to 2,200 mile range—a threat to all of the Americas.

The blockade was ordered as the United States moved swiftly to wipe out the atomic danger planted within ninety miles of Florida. On October 22, President Kennedy announced that the navy would turn back any ship carrying nuclear weapons to Cuba. The President termed it a "quarantine," because by international law a blockade is an act of war. But America was prepared to fight, Kennedy warned. He said that any missile launched from Cuba against any nation in the Western Hemisphere would be regarded as "an attack by the Soviet Union on the United States, requiring a full retaliatory response."

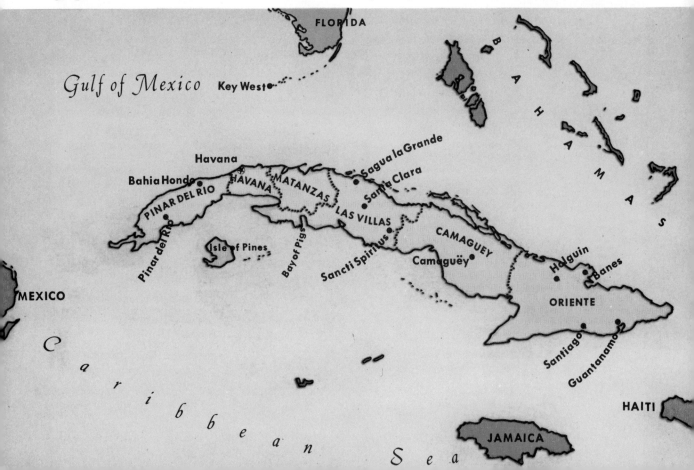

THE SOVIETS TURNED BACK from war's precipice when confronted by America's challenge. President Kennedy's blockading of Cuba was put into effect as an American armada rushed to Caribbean waters. Marines were flown to the Guantanamo naval base in Cuba. Military forces of all services were concentrated at Key West. Twenty-four reserve troop carrier air squadrons were called to active duty. The mighty aircraft carriers *Forrestal* and *Enterprise* entered the blockade zone. It was apparent that America was prepared to invade Cuba, if necessary, to destroy the missile bases.

Two ships carrying Soviet cargoes were stopped by the blockade fleet. At this point, Khrushchev offered to remove the Soviet missiles from Cuba if the United States would do likewise in Turkey. Kennedy rejected this proposal. Khrushchev abandoned bargaining and ordered the Cuban bases dismantled and

the rockets returned to Russia. Castro refused to permit United Nations inspection of the dismantling and missile removal, but Khrushchev agreed to United States inspection of Soviet ships carrying the rockets home. After their removal, Kennedy ordered the blockade lifted on November 20, 1962. He said Cuba would not be invaded as long as no further threat developed. But Castro still remained—the communist thorn in democracy's side.

The 1962 elections on November 6 were held as Cuban tension relaxed. The Democrats retained big majorities in both houses of Congress. Richard M. Nixon, former Vice-President, met bitter defeat in California as Governor Edmund G. Brown was reelected. But Republican candidates for governor won in New York, Pennsylvania, Michigan and Ohio. A new senator was elected in Massachusetts, Edward M. Kennedy—brother of the President and Attorney General.

A 22-ORBIT TRIUMPH by Major Leroy Gordon Cooper, Jr., of the Air Force convinced National Aeronautical and Space Administration officials that man could conquer problems in space. On May 15, 1963, Cooper was hurtled aloft by a giant Ajax rocket at Cape Canaveral. He rode a Mercury capsule named *Faith 7*. The next day, some 35 hours later, Cooper landed the *Faith 7* in the Pacific. He had orbited the earth 22 times. He had spent approximately 34 hours in a weightless state. He had eaten and slept well . . . and calmly and skillfully brought his mighty "bird" down to earth by manual control!

The automatic control system failed as Cooper was about to slow his 17,500-mile an hour speed and reenter the earth's atmosphere for a landing. Lieutenant Colonel John H. Glenn, America's first orbiting astronaut, was stationed on a sentinel ship in Chinese waters below. Glenn was in charge of directing landing operations. He and Cooper immediately established communication. Advised by Glenn, Cooper manually fired the "retro"

rockets to check the *Faith 7's* flight. As the capsule arched into the earth's atmosphere, Cooper guided its course by manual controls. He brought the *Faith 7* down close to the rescue aircraft carrier *Kearsarge* and was picked up. Cooper suffered no ill effects from his ordeal.

Cooper was the fourth American to go into orbit, the others being Glenn, Malcolm Scott Carpenter and Walter M. Schirra, Jr. During his 22 orbits, Cooper performed various experiments, took still and motion pictures, maneuvered the capsule, radioed messages to countries he flew over, and maintained communications with Mercury ground stations. He slept for about seven and one-half hours, and reported he was "comfortable, real comfortable." The *Faith 7* had a maximum altitude (apogee) of 165.8 miles and a low point (perigee) of 100.2 miles. Cooper and his chief ground contacts—all five of America's previous spacemen—kept up an exchange of cheerful banter. Cooper also proved man's spirits could remain high in the great outer spaces!

A BAN ON A-BOMB TESTS was put into effect by a three-power treaty signed by the United States, Great Britain and the Soviet Union. The treaty prohibited such tests in the atmosphere, in space and under water. Underground atomic tests were not prohibited. The treaty was signed in Moscow on August 5, 1963, by United States Secretary of State Dean Rusk, British Foreign Secretary Lord Home, and Soviet Foreign Minister Andrei A. Gromyko. The signing ceremony was completed in the Kremlin's palace. A joint communique was issued after the treaty was signed, stating that "this treaty is an important initial step toward the lessening of international tension and the strengthening of peace."

Some official doubt was expressed on the ban by Americans before the Senate ratified the treaty. Secretary Rusk himself warned in a speech after the signing that the pact was only a first step.

Nuclear stockpiles were not reduced, the production of nuclear weapons continued, and their use in time of war was not restricted, Rusk said. Prior to actual signing of the agreement, some members of the Senate voiced heated opposition. They cited a number of reasons. These opponents said such a seeming "ban" on A-weapons would "delude" many people into believing there no longer was any world tension, or cause to remain armed.

Another objection was raised on the grounds that the Soviet Union had done far more extensive A-weapon testing than the United States, and had exploded a 58-megaton bomb. The Soviets, the opponents pointed out, probably had outdistanced America in A-weapons, and the ban would prevent this nation from "catching up." However, after the treaty was signed, the Senate promptly ratified, and most nations of the world enthusiastically approved the nuclear arms curb.

A "FREEDOM MARCH" on Washington was staged by approximately 200,000 persons on August 28, 1963, to focus attention on Negroes' demands for equality in jobs and civil rights. The vast majority of the marchers were Negroes, but there were thousands of whites and it was estimated that 200 religious leaders — Protestant, Catholic and Jewish—joined in the demonstration. Many of the marchers traveled to Washington from as far away as the West Coast. Planes and special trains were chartered in many instances. The highways were filled with unusually heavy traffic—most of it heading for Washington.

The gathering and demonstration were completely peaceful and non-violent. This was in contrast to similar though much smaller demonstrations in other parts of the nation. In some northern cities, as well as in the deep south, chanting and marching civil rights groups frequently became involved in violence. Clashes with police were frequent, particularly in a few Southern cities. There were hundreds of arrests. The nationwide wave of protest demonstrations culminated in the Washington march. Numerous advance meetings were held, at which leaders urged a march of non-violence.

In Washington, the marchers gathered at the Washington Monument, while thirteen of their leaders called on members of Congress. Congress was considering a new civil rights law at that time. Then the marchers moved down Constitution Avenue and Independence Avenue to the Lincoln Memorial. President Kennedy commented, "The cause of 20 million Negroes has been advanced by the program before the Lincoln Memorial."

REVOLT AND A BLOODY COUP in Viet Nam ended the stormy regime of Ngo Dinh Diem and his brother, Ngo Dinh Nhu. Both lost their lives as a military group seized the government and installed a Buddhist regime. The Viet Nam problem had created international concern, and caused the American State Department particular distress. 16,000 American military advisors had volunteered for service in the war torn country. They were specially trained for fighting against guerrillas. Many American advisors piloted helicopters for the Viet Nam army as they raided behind the attacking Communist lines. Others trained Vietnamese soldiers and instructed civilians in defense. Some Americans lost their lives fighting deep in the rice fields.

The Viet Nam problem began in 1954 when the French were defeated and lost control of Viet Nam and Indo-China. Then a war caused a division of the country, the Communists taking the northern part and the anti-Communists the southern. Diem gained power and became the dictator. Meanwhile, guerrilla fighting broke out, and the United States gave the Diem forces much aid. This support was greatly curtailed when the Diem government began persecuting the Buddhists, who constitute 80 per cent of the nation's population. In protest, six Buddhist monks poured oil on their garments and set fire to themselves in public streets. Shocked and horrified, the world's sympathy swung to the Buddhists. On the afternoon of November 1, 1963, rebel troops quartered outside the city swarmed in and attacked the palace. Early on November 2, they captured it and Diem's regime of power had ended.

PRESIDENT KENNEDY WAS SLAIN by an assassin who shot him down with a sniper's rifle as the President was riding triumphantly in a motorcade in downtown Dallas. Shortly after noon on November 22, 1963, Kennedy was waving to a cheering throng from the back seat of the Presidential limousine. With him were Mrs. Jacqueline Kennedy and Texas Governor John Connally and Mrs. Nellie Connally, occupying the limousine's extra seats. All were happy and gay.

A crowd of 5,000 had greeted Kennedy warmly at the Dallas airport as he arrived from Fort Worth. Many thousands of spectators lined the motorcade's route. They waved and cheered. Kennedy waved at them. Mrs. Connally said to the President, "You can't say that Dallas isn't friendly to you today." Before Kennedy could answer, three rapid shots blasted into the car. The President slumped over the rear seat, blood streaming from a wound in the head. "Oh, no!" cried Mrs. Kennedy, gathering the limp form of her husband into her arms. Governor Connally fell to the floor of the car. One of the bullets had struck and seriously wounded the governor.

The President lived only thirty minutes. Both he and the governor were taken to Parkland hospital, but Kennedy never regained consciousness. His death was announced at 1 p.m. after last rites had been administered by a Catholic priest. A reporter and a spectator on the street said they had seen a rifle being withdrawn from a sixth floor window of a nearby warehouse building as the shots were fired. Police searching the building, found a cheap mail order rifle there, equipped with a telescopic gun sight.

KENNEDY'S LAST CAPITOL VISIT was a sad one and heart-rending to all of America. The President's body lay in state in the rotunda of the Capitol building for almost twenty-four hours, after being taken home following his assassination in Dallas. Hundreds of thousands of mourners filed past the casket throughout the day and night. Mrs. Kennedy withstood her great ordeal with dignity and courage. Returning to Washington with her husband's body on the Presidential plane, Mrs. Kennedy refused to rest. Instead, she spent the return flight alone in the compartment containing the President's coffin. She remained with the coffin as it was unloaded.

Mrs. Kennedy accompanied her dead husband to the East room of the White House, and then to the Capitol. A national day of mourning was declared for November 25, the day of the funeral. Throughout the nation, millions of Americans attended special church services. Schools, many businesses and government offices were closed. The nation mourned its dead leader, the youngest President, and the fourth to be assassinated. The other Presidents were Abraham Lincoln in 1865, James Garfield in 1881 and William McKinley in 1901.

A horror killing was witnessed on television by millions of Americans, as the suspected assassin of the President himself was murdered. Lee Harvey Oswald, a Marxist and sympathizer with Castro, was arrested as the prime suspect in the assassination. As Oswald was being transferred from the Dallas city hall to the county jail, TV cameras were turned on the scene. Viewers were horrified to see a form step out of the crowd, dart up to Oswald, thrust a gun under Oswald's heart and pull the trigger. Oswald fell dead and his slayer Jack Ruby, a night club owner, himself faced murder charges.

A HERO'S FUNERAL preceded the laying of John F. Kennedy to eternal rest in the Arlington National cemetery. Shortly before 11 a.m. on November 25, nine servicemen removed the casket from the Capitol rotunda and bore it down the steps to the waiting funeral procession. The procession went first to the White House, where Mrs. Kennedy and other members of the dead President's family left their limousines and followed behind the slowly proceeding army caisson bearing Kennedy's body. It was a black and silver caisson, drawn by six gray horses and escorted by military units. Lyndon Baines Johnson, who had been Kennedy's Vice-President, also followed the caisson. More than a million people lined the streets of Washington to view the somber, but at the same time magnificent procession bearing the dead leader.

Richard Cardinal Cushing, a personal friend of Kennedy, conducted funeral services both at St. Matthew's Cathedral and at Arlington Cemetery. After the Roman Catholic funeral mass at St. Matthews, the procession proceeded to Arlington Cemetery. Nearly 250 leaders of nations from all over the world were in the funeral procession. At Arlington, the pall bearers, their white-gloved hands moving in unison, folded to a tight triangle the flag which had covered Kennedy's coffin. Mrs. Kennedy took the flag and, hugging it, lighted an eternal blue flame at her husband's grave.

As Cardinal Cushing conducted the brief and simple graveside ceremonies, members of the President's family and more than 10,000 silent and humble citizens paid homage to the youthful and energetic 35th President. Millions of Americans watched the services on television. It was a subdued and saddened audience. The assassination of John F. Kennedy profoundly shocked America.

LYNDON BAINES JOHNSON became America's thirty-sixth President upon the death of Kennedy. Johnson, the Vice President, was sworn in as President at 2:38 p.m. on November 22, just ninety-eight minutes after Kennedy's death was announced. The swearing in ceremony took place at Dallas' Love Field in *Air Force One*, the Presidential jet plane. The plane's gold-carpeted "living room", where the ceremony took place, was crowded with twenty-seven people, including Mrs. Johnson, Mrs. Kennedy and various members of the White House staff. The short ceremony was solemn.

The first woman ever to swear in a President administered the oath of office to Johnson. She was Federal District Judge Sarah T. Hughes of Dallas, whom Kennedy had appointed to the bench on the recommendation of the then Vice-President Johnson. One other man by the name of Johnson gained the Presidency of the United States. He was Andrew Johnson, and he, too, gained office through the assassination of a President, Abraham Lincoln in a Civil War tragedy.

Lyndon Johnson, 55, had been a strong contender for the Democratic nomination for President in 1960. The party chose Kennedy, and Kennedy personally picked Johnson to be his running mate. Prior to the 1960 convention and election, Johnson was a forceful leader in the Senate from Texas. As the majority leader, he was widely respected by members of both parties. He was known as a leader who could "get things done."

"Kennedy's policies will be followed," Johnson announced shortly after taking office. Before a joint session of Congress, Johnson made an appeal for "an end to the teaching and preaching of hate and evil violence." He urged Americans in a plea for tolerance, to "turn away from the fanatics of the far left and right, from the apostles of bigotry, from those defiant of law, and those who pour venom into our nation's bloodstream."

CIGARETTE SMOKING WAS BLAMED as a cause of some fatal diseases in a report, "Smoking and Health," compiled by an advisory committee to the United States Public Health Service. The report, submitted on January 11, 1964, said, "Cigarette smoking contributes substantially to mortality from certain specific diseases and to the over-all death rate." The report stated that cigarette smoking was related to lung cancer as a cause, especially in men, outweighing all other factors. It also was described as "the most important of the causes of chronic bronchitis and increases the risk of dying from this disease." The report also connected pipe smoking with lip cancer.

The report said smoking was a greater health hazard than atmospheric pollution. It continued: "It is established that male cigarette smokers have a higher death rate from coronary (heart) disease than non-smokers." The committee's report included seven projects, in which the smoking habits of 1,123,000 men were observed over a thirteen-year period. The report said the death rate per 1,000 from all causes was sixty-eight per cent higher among smokers.

"Smoking and health" caused an immediate wave of anti-smoking sentiment across the nation. There was demand for congressional action, the most extreme being that cigarettes be outlawed, as intoxicating liquors had been during prohibition. Bills were introduced which would require tobacco companies to include warnings in their ads. Such statements as this were to be printed on cigarette packages: "Caution. Smoking may be hazardous to your health."

LYNDON B. JOHNSON WON a landslide victory in the election of 1964 to gain his first full term as President. He defeated Senator Barry Goldwater of Arizona with the greatest popular vote margin in Presidential history, 15.8 million votes. Johnson won 486 electoral votes from forty-four states, Goldwater won fifty-two electoral votes in six states. Senator Hubert Horatio Humphrey of Minnesota was elected Vice-President. Representative William Edward Miller of New York was Goldwater's running mate for Vice-President.

A white backlash which had been expected by some as a result of the civil rights movement failed to develop, except in the deep South. Alabama, Georgia, Louisiana, Mississippi and South Carolina went for Goldwater, his home state of Arizona being his only other victory. America's largest number of voters in history went to the polls—42,670,000. Johnson's plurality exceeded Franklin Delano Roosevelt's previous record winning margin of 11,072,000 (in 1936) and the total vote surpassed the former record of 35,585,000 (1956 Eisenhower election.)

The democratic platform promised to make America the most powerful nation on earth, back civil rights to the fullest, extend wage minimums, press for medicare, and repeal section 14(b) of the Taft Hartley labor act, which permitted states to outlaw the union shop. The Republicans backed civil rights and pledged to cut government spending, extend social security, and provide full medicare for the aged.

GREATER RIGHTS FOR NEGROES were guaranteed by the Civil Rights Act of 1964, which became law on July 2. The new act called for equal treatment in employment, voting and public accommodations. In some respects the new act merely stated again principles laid down in previous civil rights laws. A major new provision was that Negroes were to be given equal service in such public accommodations as hotels, restaurants, theatres and public transportation. All voting rights of Negroes were to be respected. A later voting rights law gave the Attorney General the authority to assign federal registrars to supervise the registration of Negro voters in states where there was evidence of any discrimination.

Civil rights strife across the nation soon followed. Mass demonstrations by civil rights workers took place not only in the South but in such northern cities as New York, Chicago and Philadelphia. The Reverend Dr. Martin Luther King was a movement leader.

King led demonstrations in Selma, Alabama, which lasted for three months, beginning on January 2, 1965. There were several killings, including the murder of Mrs. Viola Gregg Liuzzo, a white civil worker from Detroit, near Selma on March 25. Previously, three civil rights workers, two white and one Negro, were slain in Mississippi. Thirty-five, including police, were killed in riots in the Watts Negro district of Los Angeles in August, 1965.

MARS WAS PHOTOGRAPHED by the American satellite *Mariner IV*, giving this nation a new space triumph and providing man with his first close-up views of the red planet. The *Mariner IV* traveled 350 million miles in eight months after its launching on November 28, 1964, to approach within a clear photographing distance of 10,500 miles on July 15, 1965. After a 4,000-mile sweep past three deserts, an "oasis" and Mars' south polar cap, *Mariner IV* transmitted its pictures to Earth across 135 million miles of space, having circled to intercept Mars in its orbit.

Mariner IV was equipped with automatic telephoto equipment, which transmitted its photographs in the manner of the newspaper facsimile process—by television. Eight pieces of each picture were transmitted in one second. The photo was sent one line at a time, 200 lines joining to form one picture. The first photo required eight hours and thirty-five minutes for transmission. It clearly showed craters on Mars and revealed atmosphere so thin that man could not live there without pressurized suits. No evidence of life on Mars was shown. Mars still remained a mystery for man to solve.

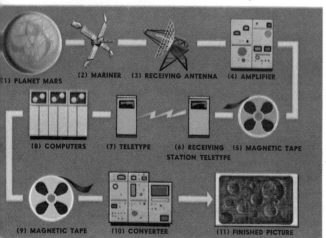

(1) PLANET MARS (2) MARINER (3) RECEIVING ANTENNA (4) AMPLIFIER

(8) COMPUTERS (7) TELETYPE (6) RECEIVING STATION TELETYPE (5) MAGNETIC TAPE

(9) MAGNETIC TAPE (10) CONVERTER (11) FINISHED PICTURE

A PERILOUS WALK IN SPACE was the feat accomplished by American astronaut Edward H. White on June 3, 1965. Orbiting the earth in *Gemini 4,* with James McDivitt as command pilot, White stepped from the capsule and for twenty-one minutes maneuvered in the hostile void of space—in the manner of a human satellite. He wore a pressure suit filled with oxygen, fed by a twenty-five foot umbilical cord attached to the capsule. White propelled himself around the spacecraft with a hand thruster rocket "gun." He braved the dangers of "space bullets," deadly meteorites flashing by.

McDivitt took photographs of White in his walk, urging, "Hey, Ed, smile." The astronaut traveled nearly a quarter of the way around the world during his stroll. He was exhilarated, White said later, adding "It was the saddest moment of my life when McDivitt ordered me back inside the capsule." But White had verified that man could step out of a spacecraft, maneuver, and return safely to his cabin. Before the walk, *Gemini 4* failed in an effort to rendezvous with the orbiting second stage of its Titan 2 rocket.

THE DEATH OF ADLAI STEVENSON

on July 14, 1965, saddened America. Tributes from all over the world came to the man who twice had been a candidate for President of the United States. At the time of his death, Stevenson was America's ambassador to the United Nations. He was on a U.N. mission in Europe when he collapsed and died on the sidewalk outside the United States embassy in London. Mrs. Ronald Tree, United States delegate to the U.N. Trusteeship council, was with Stevenson at the time. She tried unsuccessfully to revive him. He was sixty-five years old at his death.

A delegation headed by Stevenson's three sons—Adlai III, John Fell and Borden—and Vice President Humphrey brought Stevenson home for burial. After lying in state in Washington and Springfield, Stevenson was buried in his family's home town of Bloomington, Illinois. It was a sad farewell for Illinois, where Adlai Ewing Stevenson once had been governor and for years a state leader.

Arthur J. Goldberg, Supreme Court Justice, on July 20 was appointed to succeed Stevenson as the U.N. Ambassador. Goldberg had been on the Supreme Court since his appointment in August, 1962. Prior to then, he had been Kennedy's Secretary of Labor.

WAR IN VIET NAM GREW more violent on two fronts—military and political. Both the American-supported South Vietnamese and the Communist Viet Cong built up their forces steadily as the fighting became more widespread. In April, 1966, Secretary of Defense Robert S. McNamara reported that the United States had the greatest military strength of any nation in history. America's force in Viet Nam numbered 335,000, McNamara said, including 60,000 men patrolling the China Sea aboard the Seventh Fleet.

United States Marines and soldiers, aided by South Vietnamese and supported by helicopters, pressed continuous ground attacks against the Viet Cong. Air Force and Marine planes from bases in South Viet Nam, huge B-52 bombers from Guam, and Navy carrier planes heavily bombed the war areas, including missile sites and military targets in North Viet Nam. Viet Cong guerrillas repeatedly set off bombs in American installations and troop billets in Saigon. American casualties mounted into the thousands.

Since the assassination of Ngo Dinh Diem on January 30, 1964, South Viet Nam had tried eight governments. Many were military administrations.

ALL SPACE ENDURANCE records were shattered by two American astronauts, Commander Gordon Cooper, Jr., and Charles (Pete) Conrad. They orbited the earth 120 times in a continuous eight-day flight which lasted from blast-off on August 21, 1965, to splashdown on August 29. They traveled 3,338,200 miles in their spacecraft, *Gemini 5*. They encountered major difficulties, but overcame them all. Early in the flight problems developed in the fuel cells due to faulty oxygen and water distribution. *Gemini 5* went into a period of tumbling entering the eighth day of the flight, but by manual maneuvering the astronauts brought their spacecraft under normal control.

Neither Cooper nor Conrad could bathe or shave during the flight. But they slept regularly and ate three meals, in addition to snacks, each day. Their diet included cereal, bacon, eggs, cubes of toast, beef, gravy, corn, fruit cake and orange juice. Each meal cost more than $200, due to the intricate process of freezing, compressing and dehydrating. Much of the food was reconstructed with water. The concentrated cubes could be taken in a single bite.

On one of their orbits, Cooper and Conrad watched a Minuteman missile which had been fired from the Vandenburg air base in California. They reported having seen "beautiful views" of the earth as they circled overhead. They "splashed" 600 miles east of Jacksonville, Florida, both wearing heavy beards which, nevertheless, could not hide winners' smiles.

A

ABC powers: mediate Mexican trouble, 10-791

Abolitionists: Movement in North, 5-336; gain in strength, 5-360; methods of: 6-409; leaders, 6-411, 460; and Uncle Tom's Cabin, 6-415; aid to Kansas, 6-426, 434; and John Brown, 6-457, 458

Accessory Transit Company: 6-432

Acheson, Dean: and North Atlantic Treaty Organization, 15-1155; in Korean War "Great Debate," 15-1167; discusses German questions, 15-1170

Adams, Charles Francis: American minister to England, 7-495

Adams, John: on Writs of Assistance, 2-98; and Boston Massacre, 2-113; in treaty negotiations with England, 2-154; minister to England, 3-173; elected Vice-President, 3-204; elected President, 3-213; in election of 1800, 3-225; pardons Fries, 4-252; death of, 4-311

Adams, John Quincy: minister to Russia, 4-284; Secretary of State, 4-295, 301; defends Jackson 4-299; in 1820 election, and Latin America, 4-306; sixth President, 4-309; and Panama Congress, 4-311; defeated for reelection, 4-315; on right of petition, 5-349, 357

Adams, Samuel: organizes Committee of Correspondence, 2-116

Adamson Act: shortens railroad working hours, 11-822

Addams, Jane: founds Hull House, 9-672

Adet, Pierre August: 3-213

Adjusted Compensation Act: provides bonus payments to veterans, 13-1003

Africa: Moors in, 1-10; Portuguese, 1-16; slave trade, 1-45; Triangular Trade, 2-107; World War II campaign, 14-1080; 1082, 1086

Agramonte, Aristides: 9-713

Agricultural Adjustment Act: provides aid for farmers, 13-974; declared unconstitutional, 13-1002; second law passed (1938), 13-1019

Agricultural Credits Act: 12-930

Agricultural Marketing Act: attempts to alleviate farm depression, 12-931

Agriculture, Department of: established, 7-512; raised to Cabinet status, 9-678

Aguinaldo, Emilio: Filipino patriot aids Americans, 9-704; rebels against United States, 9-706

Air Commerce Act: places civil aviation under Secretary of Commerce, 12-914

Airlift: relieves Berlin, 15-1147

Airmail: development of 12-914

Alabama: Confederate sea raider preys on Northern shipping, 7-509; loss of, 7-546; and settlement of claims, 8-602

Alamance, Battle of: rebellion of "Regulators" in North Carolina, 2-114

Alamo: siege of, 5-351-352

Alaska: discovery, 1-73; purchased from Russia, 8-583; and discovery of gold, 9-694, and Panhandle boundary dispute, 10-747; admitted as a state, 16-1222

Albany Plan of Union: Franklin's idea for colonial cooperation, 2-95

Albemarle: Confederate ship, 7-539

Aldrich, Nelson W.: 10-771

Aleutian Islands: discovery, 1-73; in World War II, 14-1079, 1094

Alexander VI, Pope: establishes Line of Demarcation, 1-16

Alexander I, Czar of Russia: aids Napoleon's blockade of England, 4-260; offers to mediate War of 1812, 4-284

Algeciras, Act of: 10-756

Algonquin Indians: 1-40

Alien Act (1798): passed by Congress, 3-218; becomes issue in states' rights, 3-219; issue in campaign of 1800, 3-226

Alien and Sedition Acts: 3-218, 219, 226

Alien Registration Act (1940): 14-1053

Allen, Ethan: at Ticonderoga, 2-124

Altgeld, John P.: frees Haymarket prisoners, 9-660; refuses troops in Pullman strike, 9-690

Amendments, Constitutional: First to Tenth (Bill of Rights), 3-196-197; Twelfth, 4-254; Thirteenth, 8-570; Fourteenth, 8-575, 10-753; Fifteenth, 8-598; Sixteenth, 10-783; Seventeenth, 10-787; Eighteenth, 11-857; Nineteenth, 11-870; Twentieth, 13-982; Twenty-first, 13-983; Twenty-second, 15-1176

American Dictionary of the English Language: 4-313

American Expeditionary Force (A.E.F.): first American troops arrive in France, 11-841; operates as separate army at Pershing's insistence, 11-846; stops German drive on Paris, 11-847; in heavy fighting at Belleau Wood, 11-848; stems German offensive of March, 1918, 11-850; in first independent American action at St. Mihiel, 11-851; in Meuse-Argonne offensive 11-852

American Federation of Labor (A.F. of L.): founded, 9-663; and Samuel Gompers, 12-910; and struggle over industrial unions, 13-998; merges with CIO, 15-1189

American Legion: founded, 11-859; agitates for soldiers' bonus, 12-904

American System: 4-308

Ames, Oakes: 8-606

Amistad Incident: slave revolt, 5-364

Ampudia, General Pedro de: in Mexican War, 5-381

Anderson, Richard C.: 4-311

Anderson, Major Robert: and Fort Sumter, 6-475; 7-492

Andersonville: cruelty at Confederate prison, 7-555

Andre, Major John: conspires with Arnold, 2-149

Anthony, Susan B.: pleads for women's suffrage, 6-460; 8-593

Antietam, Battle of: 7-515

Anti-Masonic Party: 5-337

Anti-Saloon League: 10-731

Anzus: mutual assistance alliance in Pacific, 15-1173

Apache Indians: 1-64; war with, 9-674

Arabic: sinking of liner brings German pledge, 11-814

Arabs: oppose State of Israel, 15-1146; United Arab Republic formed, 16-1216

Argentina: in Venezuelan debt question, 10-745; refuses to break with Axis, 14-1074; and admission to United Nations, 14-1109

Arizona: admitted as state, 10-777

Arkwright, Richard: 3-188

Armada, Spanish: 1-38

Armstrong, John: 4-278

Arnold, General Benedict: at Ticonderoga, 2-124; betrays Washington, 2-149

Aroostook War: Canadian-American boundary dispute, 5-363; settled, 5-374

Arthur, Chester A.: dismissed as customs collector, 8-632; Vice-Presidential candidate, 8-634; elected, 8-635; assumes Presidency after Garfield's assassination, 9-652

Articles of Confederation: adopted by Second Continental Congress, 2-143; ratified, 2-153; shortcomings of, 3-176

Astor, John Jacob: organizes fur trading companies, 4-263

Atahualpa, Inca Emperor of Peru: 1-27

Atlanta, Georgia: 7-537

Atlantic Charter: outline of war aims, 14-1066

Atomic Bomb Tests: banned, 16-1258

Attlee, Clement R.: at Potsdam Conference, 14-1113

Atomic Bomb: Einstein advises development by America, 13-1019; exploded, 14-1112; dropped on Japan, 14-1114; Russia explodes, 15-1158

Atomic energy: control of, 15-1132, 1183

Atomic Energy Commission: 15-1132, 1183

"Atoms for Peace" plan: 15-1193

Attorney General: heads Department of Justice, 8-601

Aurora 7: Mercury space capsule orbits earth three times, 16-1241

Austria: annexed by Germany, 13-1020

Austria-Hungary: and causes of World War I, 11-808-809; and peace treaty of World War I, 12-891

Aztec Indians: 1-23

B

Bacon, Nathaniel: leads rebellion in Virginia, 1-66

Badoglio, Marshal Pietro: 14-1090

Baghdad Pact: 15-1188

Bagot, Charles: 4-297

Bainbridge, Captain William: 4-279

Balboa, Vasco Nunez de: 1-21

Balkans: and causes of World War I, 11-808-809; invaded by Axis, 14-1059

Ballard, Guy: heads religious movement, 13-1027

Ballinger, Richard A: in conservation dispute, 10-772-773

Baltimore, Lord Cecilius Calvert: founds Maryland, 1-53; quarrels with Penn, 1-67

Bank holiday of 1933: 13-970

Bank of the United States: established, 3-194; and expiration of charter, 4-269; re-chartered, 4-294; and Panic of 1819, 4-300; and Supreme Court ruling, 4-302; opposed by Jackson, 5-329; as issue in campaign of 1832, 5-340; closes, 5-354

Baranov, Alexander A.: 3-221

Barbary pirates: attack American ships and exact tribute, 3-181, 230; defeated by Americans, 4-250, 293

Barkley, Alben W.: 15-1152

Barnett, Ross: acts in University of Mississippi integration crisis, 16-1243

Barron, Commodore James: 4-257

Bartholdi, Frederic A.: creates Statue of Liberty, 9-662

Bartlett, E. L.: 16-1222

Barton, Clara: serves as Union nurse in Civil War, 7-541

Baruch, Bernard M.: heads World War I War Industries Board, 11-839; in Cold war, 15-1132, 15-1149

Batista, Fulgencio: defeated by Castro, 16-1220

Battle Hymn of the Republic: popular Civil War song, 7-502

Bayard, James A.: peace commissioner, 4-284

Beard, Daniel C.: in Boy Scout movement, 10-774

Beauregard General Pierre: leads attack on Fort Sumter, **7**-492; and First Battle of Bull Run, **7**-497

Beecher, Henry Ward: and Beecher's Bibles, **6**-434

Beecher, Lyman: temperance leader, **5**-395

Belgium: invaded by Germany in World War I, **10**-793, **11**-809; attacked by Germany in World War II, **14**-1050

Belknap, William W.: in Grant scandals, **8**-618

Bell, Alexander Graham: invents telephone **8**-619

Bell, John: **6**-464, 471

Belleau Wood, Battle of: **11**-848

Bering, Vitus: explores North America, **1**-73

Bering Sea: discovered by Vitus Bering, **1**-73; and sealing controversy, **9**-686

Berkeley, Sir William: governor of Virginia, **1**-66

Berlin: in Cold War, **16**-1240

Berlin Blockade: **15**-1147

Berlin Wall: **16**-1247

Bernadotte, Count Folke: **15**-1146

Bernstorff, Johann von: activities in World War I, **11**-814, 817, 829

Bessemer, Sir Henry: discovers steel making process, **6**-433

Bevin, Ernest: **15**-1143

Biddle, Nicholas: and Bank of the United States, **5**-340, 343

Billings, Warren K.: and Preparedness Day bombing, **11**-823

Billings, William: early songwriter, **2**-106

Bismarck Sea, Battle of: **14**-1094

Bissell, George H.: **6**-456

Black Codes: restrictions on Negroes, **8**-572

"Black Friday": starts business panic of 1869, **8**-595

Black Hawk War: **5**-339

Blackwell, Elizabeth: first woman physician, **5**-395

Black Warrior: Cuban seizure of American ship, **6**-430

Blaine, James G.: loses Republican nomination, **8**-622; in 1880 Convention, **8**-634; leads "Half-Breeds," **9**-650; leaves Cabinet, **9**-652; nominated for President, **9**-656; and Campaign of 1884, **9**-657; and First Pan-American Conference, **9**-673; in sealing controversy, **9**-686

Blanchard, Pierre: makes first balloon ascent, **3**-200

Bland-Allison Act: restores silver coinage. **8**-630

Bliss, Tasker H.: **11**-856

"Blitzkrieg": German lightning warfare strikes, **14**-1050-1052, 1059, 1064

Blondin, the Great: walks tightrope across Niagara Falls, **6**-455

Bloomer, Amelia: **6**-460

Blount, William: expelled from Senate, **3**-215

Bolivar, Simon: South American leader, **4**-306; calls Panama Congress, **4**-311

Bonhomme Richard: defeats British ship Serapis, **2**-148

Bonus Act: **12**-904

Bonus march: fails to achieve veterans' aims, **12**-950

Boone, Daniel: **2**-112

Booth, John Wilkes: assassinates Lincoln, **7**-551; death of, **7**-553

Borah, William E.: opposes League of Nations, **11**-862; and Kellogg-Briand Pact, **12**-924

Boston: evacuated by British, **2**-131; and police strike of 1919, **11**-865

Boston Latin School: **1**-54

Boston Massacre: **2**-113

Boston News-Letter: early American newspaper, **1**-71

Boston Tea Party: **2**-117

Bougainville: won by Americans, **14**-1094

Bowles, Chester: **15**-1131

Boxer Rebellion: anti-foreign revolt in China, **9**-712

Boy Scouts of America: **10**-774

Bradford, William: governor of Plymouth, **1**-49; writes History of New England, **1**-72

Brady, Matthew B.: Civil War photographer, **7**-526

"Brain Trust": **13**-969

Brandy Station, Battle of: **7**-520

Brandywine, Battle of: **2**-141

Brazil, becomes Portuguese, **1**-16; reached by Vespucci, **1**-19; cooperates in fighting Axis, **14**-1074

Breckinridge, John C.: in 1856 election, **6**-437; in 1860 election, **6**-470-471

Bretton Woods Conference: International Monetary Fund created, **14**-1098

Briand, Aristide: **12**-924

Bristow, Benjamin H.: unearths Whiskey Ring corruption, **8**-616

British Guiana: boundary dispute with Venezuela, **9**-709

Brock, General Isaac: in War of 1812, **4**-276, 277

Broke, Captain P.B.V.: **4**-280

Brooklyn Bridge: opened in 1883, **9**-655

Brooks, Preston S.: **6**-435

Brown, Major General Jacob: takes Fort Erie, **4**-286; in Battle of Lundy Lane, **4**-287

Brown, John: and Pottawatomie massacre, **6**-436, 476; at Harper's Ferry, **6**-457, 476; hanged, **6**-458

Brussels Pact (1948): **15**-1145

Bryan, William Jennings: delivers "Cross of Gold" speech, **9**-693; loses in 1896 election, **9**-695; supports Treaty of Paris, **9**-705; loses in 1900 election, **9**-714; loses in 1908 election, **10**-766; as Wilson's Secretary of State, **10**-786; favors neutrality, **10**-793; resignation of, **11**-813; in evolution trial, **12**-911

Bryan-Chamorro Treaty: gives United States rights in Nicaragua, **11**-818

Bryant, William Cullen: American poet, **7**-544

Buchanan, James: minister to England, **6**-430; fifteenth President, **6**-437; and Kansas, **6**-438; in 1858 elections, **6**-450; blocks slave trade, **6**-454; and Fort Sumter, **6**-475

Buckner, General Simon B. Jr.: in Battle of Okinawa, **14**-1107

Budget and Accounting Act: creates national Bureau of the Budget, **12**-890

Bulganin, Nikolai: at Summit meeting. **15**-1187

Bulgaria: joins Axis, **14**-1059

Bulge, Battle of the: **14**-1101

Bull Run, First Battle of: **7**-497; Second Battle of, **7**-513

Bunau-Varilla, Philippe: encourages revolt in Panama, **10**-748

Bunche, Ralph J.: arranges Arab-Israeli armistice, **15**-1146

Bunker Hill, Battle of: **2**-128

Burgesses, House of: **1**-46

Burgoyne, General John: **2**-141, 142

Burke-Wadsworth Selective Training and Service Act: **14**-1057

Burlingame, Anson: negotiates treaty with China, **8**-590; modification of treaty, **9**-680

Burnside, General Ambrose E.: defeated at Fredericksburg and replaced by Hooker, **7**-516

Burr, Aaron: candidate for President, **3**-213; elected Vice-President, **3**-225; and duel with Hamilton, **4**-253; tried for treason, **4**-256

Bushnell, David: invents first submarine, **2**-137

Butler, Andrew P.: **6**-435

Butler, General Benjamin F.: occupies New Orleans, **7**-508

Byrd, Richard E.: makes first flight over North Pole, **12**-915; flies over South Pole, **12**-934

Byrnes, James F.: heads Office of War Mobilization, **14**-1088; as United Nations delegate, **15**-1130; and foreign relief, **15**-1135

C

Cabinet: development of, **3**-186

Cabot, George: **4**-291

Cabot, John: **1**-18, 19

Cabot, Sebastian: **1**-18, 19

Cabral, Pedro: **1**-11

Cadore, Duc de: **4**-267

Cairo Conferences: **14**-1093

Caldwell, Erskine: American writer, **13**-1026

Calhoun, John C.: member of War Hawks, **4**-271; favors national bank, **4**-294; as Secretary of War, **4**-295, 304; and Bonus Bill, **4**-296; elected Vice-President, **4**-309; writes South Carolina Exposition, **4**-314; reelected, **4**-315; defends states' rights, **5**-332, in Eaton Affair, **5**-335; breaks with Jackson, **5**-340; upholds nullification,

5-341; resigns as Vice-President, **5**-342; opposes Wilmot Proviso, **5**-384; pleads for South, **5**-396; death of, **6**-421

California: Drake claims for England, **1**-34; in Mexican War, **5**-386; ceded to United States, **5**-389; and discovery of gold, **5**-391; gold rush, **5**-392; admitted to Union, **5**-396; and mining camps, **6**-412; Chinese labor problem, **8**-628, **9**-680; Japanese labor problem, **10**-764; population gain, **16**-1232

California Workingmen's Party: **8**-628

Callender, James T.: **4**-252

Cameron, Simon: appointed Secretary of War, **7**-491; replaced by Stanton, **7**-501

Canada: early explorations: **1**-28, 40; in War of 1812, **4**-275, 278; and Klondike boundary dispute, **10**-747; protection under Monroe Doctrine, **13**-1034

Canals: **6**-423, 429

Canary Islands: **1**-14

Canning, George: **4**-306

Cannon, Joseph G.: **10**-771

Cantigny, Battle of: **11**-848

Cape of Good Hope: in era of exploration, **1**-11, 17, 34

Cape Verde Islands: **1**-16

Carnegie, Andrew: steel magnate in philanthropic causes, **10**-729, 737

Carnegie Steel Company: and strike violence, **9**-681

Caroline Affair: Canadian border incident, **5**-361

Carpenter, Lt. Comdr. Malcolm Scott: orbits earth three times **16**-1242

"Carpetbaggers": seek private gain in South, **8**-569, 589, 599

Carranza, Venustiano: **10**-791; **11**-815, 820

Carroll, James: **9**-713

Carson, Kit: **5**-373

Cartier, Jacques: in Canada, **1**-28

Casablanca Conference: **14**-1083

Castlereagh, Lord: **4**-284

Castro, Cipriano: Venezuelan dictator, **10**-744

Castro, Fidel: assumes power in Cuba, **16**-1220; and actions leading to U.S. break, **16**-1233; blockade by United States, **16**-1245; and crisis of 1962, **16**-1245, 1246

Catherine II (The Great), Empress of Russia: makes Russia's first claim to American territory, **3**-221

Caucus system: in election of 1800, **3**-225

Census: first official count (1790), **3**-191; census of 1800, **3**-227; of 1840, **5**-366; of 1850, **5**-394; of 1860, **6**-476; of 1870, **8**-600; of 1880, **8**-635; of 1890, **9**-674; of 1920, **11**-876; of 1930, **12**-940; of 1940, **13**-1036; of 1950, **15**-1168; of 1960, **16**-1232

Central Intelligence Agency: **15**-1141

Central Pacific Railroad: joins with

C (contd.)

Union Pacific Railroad to complete trancontinental route, 8·594

Century of Progress Exposition (1933): World's Fair at Chicago, Illinois, 13·976

Cermak, Anton: assassinated, 13·968

Cervera, Admiral Pascual: at Santiago, 9·702

Chamberlain, Neville: and Munich Pact, 13·1024; and Polish guarantee, 13·1028; resigns, 14·1050

Chambers, Whittaker: 15·1151

Champlain, Samuel de: 1·40

Chancellorsville, Battle of: 7·519

Charles I, King of England: 1·46, 58

Charles II, King of England: 1·61

Chase, Salmon P.: appointed Secretary of Treasury, 7·491; presides at impeachment trial of President Johnson, 8·587

Chase, Samuel: and trial of Fries, 3·220; impeachment of 4·252

Chateau-Thierry, Battle of: 11·847

Chattanooga, Battle of: 7·524, 527

Chauncey, Captain Isaac: 4·283

Chesapeake-Leopard affair: 4·257

Cheves, Langdon: 4·271

Chiang Kai-shek: resists Japanese, 14·1049; at Cairo Conference, 14·1093; flees to Formosa, 15·1159; and offshore islands, 16·1217

Chicago: fire of 1871, 8·604, World's Fair, 9·684; Century of Progress, 13·976; as inland port, 16·1221

Chickamauga, Battle of: 7·524

Chile: refuses to break with Axis, 14·1074

China: and early American trade, 3·171, 193; signs treaties with United States, 6·446; and immigration, 8·590; and Open Door notes, 9·708; in Boxer Rebellion, 9·712; becomes republic, 10·786; in Washington Conference, 12·895; and invasion of Manchuria by Japan, 12·945; and attack in North, 13·1013; and Yalta Conference, 14·1104; as permanent member of Security Council, 15·1130; receives aid, 15·1135; falls to Communists, 15·1159; and Communist action in Korea, 15·1165-1166; and offshore islands, 15·1178, 16·1217

Chinese Exclusion Act: 9·680

Chinese labor: becomes problem in American West, 8·628

Chou En-lai: 15·1165, 1178

Churchill, Winston: soldier and statesman, 14·1048; becomes prime minister, 14·1050; and Battle of Britain, 14·1055; and Atlantic Charter, 14·1066; at Quebec Conference, 14·1092; at Teheran and Cairo Conferences, 14·1093; at Yalta Conference, 14·1104

Church of England: 1·47

Cibola, Seven Cities of: 1·30

Cigarette smoking: report by Public

Health Service, 16·1255

Cinque: leads revolt of slaves, 5·364

Civilian Conservation Corps: aids unemployed youth, 13·971

Civil Rights Act: (1866) gives citizenship to Negroes, 8·573; (1875) broadens rights for Negroes, 8·613; (1957) creates commission, 16·1210; (1964) extends rights for Negroes, 16·1257

Civil Service: and reforms in Pendleton Act, 9·654

Civil Service Commission: 8·632

Civil War: 7·488-556

Civil Works Administration: 13·981

Clark, George Rogers: in Northwest Expedition, 2·146

Clark, General Mark: in invasion of Italy, 14·1090

Clark, William: explores West, 4·251

Clark Memorandum: modifies Roosevelt Corollary to Monroe Doctrine, 12·928

Clay, Henry: as War Hawk, 4·271; favors national bank, 4·294; and Missouri Compromise, 4·303; favors recognition of Latin-American republics, 4·306; and American System, 4·308; as Secretary of State, 4·309; nominated for President, 5·340; formulates tariff compromise, 5·342; censures Jackson, 5·343; resigns from Senate, 5·371; again nominated for President, 5·379; proposes compromise on slavery, 5·396; death of, 6·421

Clay, General Lucius D.: 15·1143, 1149

Clayton Anti-Trust Act: 10·796

Clayton-Bulwer Treaty: on Central American canal, 5·393; 6·429; 10·736

Clemenceau, Georges: at Paris peace conference, 11·856

Clermont: first successful steamboat, 4·258; 5·334

Cleveland, Grover: nominated for President, 9·656; character attacked in election of 1884, 9·657; elected President, 9·658; dedicates Statue of Liberty, 9·662; acts on Confederate flag question and Civil War pensions, 9·666; defeated in election of 1888, 9·667; again becomes President, 9·682; recognizes Hawaiian republic, 9·683; sends troops in Pullman strike, 9·690; and gold purchases, 9·692; in Venezuelan boundary dispute, 9·709

Clinton, De Witt: in 1812 election, 4·274; sponsors Erie Canal, 4·310

Clinton, George: 4·254, 264

Clinton, General Henry: 2·144, 149, 150

Clipper Ships: 6·423

Coast Guard: in World War II, 14·1089; womens unit (SPARS), 14·1084

Colfax, Schuyler: 8·591

Colombia: 10·742, 748; 15·1150

Colorado: and discovery of gold, 6·452

Colt, Samuel: invents repeater pistol, 5·348

Columbia, South Carolina: burned and evacuated, 7·547

Columbia: trading vessel, 3·193

Columbian Exposition (1893): World's Fair at Chicago, Illinois, 9·684

Columbia River: 3·199

Columbus, Christopher: wins Queen Isabella's support, 1·13; voyages, 1·14, 15

Comanche Indians: 1·64

Command of the Army Act: 8·580, 586

Commerce and Labor, Department of: created, 10·746

Commerce, Department of: separate cabinet office created, 10·785

Committee for Industrial Organization: splits from A.F. of L., 12·998

Committee of Fifteen: 8·575, 577

Committee on Public Information: censorship and propaganda agency in World War I, 11·838

Committee on Un-American Activities: 15·1151

Committees of Correspondence: 2·116, 119

Common Sense: written by Thomas Paine, 2·130

Compromise of 1850: 5·396

Comptroller General: heads General Accounting Office, 12·890

Comstock Lode: 6·453

Concord, Battle of: 2·122, 123

Confederate battle flag controversy: 9·666

Confederate States of America: provisional government formed, 7·490; capital established at Richmond, Virginia, 7·493; war strategy, 7·499; final surrender, 7·552

Congress: first meeting of, 3·184

Congress of Industrial Organizations: becomes rival of A.F. of L., 13·1025; merges with A.F. of L., 15·1189

Conkling, Roscoe: 8·634; 9·650

Connally, Tom: 15·1130

Connecticut, Fundamental Orders of: 1·57

Conquistadors: 1·23, 31

Conrad, Charles (Pete): orbits earth, 16·1262

Conservation: fostered by Newlands Reclamation and Forest Reserve Acts, 10·741; spurred by 1908 conference, 10·765; and controversy in Taft Administration, 10·772-773

Constitutional Union Party: 6·464

Constitution of the United States: provisions, 3·180; ratified, 3·183; see Amendments, Constitutional

Continental Associations: formed by colonists to boycott British trade, 2·119, 121

Continental Congress: First (1774),

2·119; Second (1775), 2·125

Conway Plot: attempt to replace Washington as commander, 2·144

Cooke, Jay: and Panic of 1873, 8·611

Coolidge, Calvin: acts in Boston police strike, 11·865; nominated for Vice-President, 11·869; elected, 11·871; becomes President, 12·899; wins in election of 1924, 12·908; favors naval disarmament, 12·918; and peace pact, 12·924; chooses not to run for President, 12·926

Cooper, Major Leroy Gordon: orbits earth, 16·1247; breaks space record, 16·1262

Cooper, Peter: builds first locomotive, 5·334

Copley, John Singleton: artist, 2·106

Copyright, law of: 3·192

Coral Sea, Battle of: 14·1078

Corbin, Abel R.: 8·595

Cornwallis, Lord Charles: 2·138, 150, 151

Coronado, Francisco Vasquez de: 1·30

Corregidor: falls to Japanese, 14·1071

Cortez, Hernando: conquers Aztecs, 1·23; falls into disfavor, 1·24; and Pizarro, 1·27

Cotton: and effect on South, 3·203

Cotton gin: invented, 3·203

Coughlin, Charles E.: 13·1006

Council on Foreign Ministers: 14·1113, 1116; 15·1136, 1143

Council of National Defense: in World War I, 11·822

Cowpens, Battle of: 2·150

Cox, James M.: nominated for President, 11·869; defeated, 11·871

Coxey, Jacob S.: leader of unemployed demonstrators, 9·689

"Coxey's Army": march of unemployed on Washington, D. C., 9·689

Cramer, Charles F.: 12·906

Crawford, William H.: in 1816 election, 4·295; Secretary of Treasury, 4·304; in 1824 election, 4·309

Credit Mobilier: corrupt railroad scheme, 8·606

Creek Indians: 4·285

Creel, George: heads wartime information bureau, 11·838

Creole Affair: slave ship mutiny, 5·369

"Crime of 1873": demonetization of silver, 8·608

Cripple Creek, Colorado: miners' strike, 9·688

Crittenden, John J.: proposes slavery compromise, 6·473

Crittenden, Colonel William L.: 6·413

Crockett, Davy: 5·352

Crown Point, Battle of: 2·124

Crusades: causes of exploration, 1·9

Cuba: discovered by Columbus, 1·15; as Spanish stronghold, 1·31; and Lopez invasion, 6·413, 430; and Ostend Manifesto, 6·430; in revolt

C (contd.)

against Spain, **8**-612, **9**-697; given up by Spain, **9**-705; gains self-rule, **10**-733, 738; and Good Neighbor Policy, **13**-984; taken over by Castro, **16**-1220; and U.S. break, **16**-1233; repels invasion, **16**-1236; and blockade by United States, **16**-1245, 1246

Cuban National Revolutionary Council: **16**-1242

Cultural developments: in colonies, 1-72, **2**-106; Civil War period writers, **7**-544; at close of Nineteenth Century, **9**-716; in the 1920's, **12**-935; during the Great Depression, **13**-1026, 1027; at Mid-Twentieth Century, **15**-1169

Cumberland Road: opens travel to the west, **4**-298

Cuming, Alfred: **6**-451

Curtis, Charles: **12**-926

Cushing, Caleb: first American commissioner to China, **5**-378

Cushing, Lieutenant William B.: destroys Confederate ship Albemarle, **7**-539

Custer, General George A.: and Mosby's Raiders, **7**-536; in last stand at Little Big Horn, **8**-623

Czechoslovakia: loses Sudetenland to Germany, **13**-1024; annexed by Hitler, **13**-1028; becomes Russian satellite, **15**-1144

Czolgosz, Leon: assassinates President McKinley, **10**-734

D

Dame schools: 1-54

Danbury Hatters Case: Supreme Court rules against labor union, **10**-763

Dare, Virginia: 1-37

Darlan, Admiral Jean: **14**-1082, 1083

Darrow, Clarence: in evolution trial, **12**-911

Dartmouth College versus Woodward: Supreme Court rules on contracts, **4**-302

Daugherty, Harry M.: in Harding scandals, **12**-906

Daughters of the American Revolution: **9**-677

Davis, Elmer: **14**-1075

Davis, Jefferson: urges resumption of slave trade, **6**-454; defends slavery, **6**-459; elected President of Confederacy, **7**-490; issues call to arms, **7**-493; captured, **7**-552; receives pardon, **8**-592

Davis, John W.: loses in election of 1924, **12**-908

Dawes, Charles G.: appointed first Director of Bureau of Budget, **12**-890; and war debt plan, **12**-903; elected Vice-President, **12**-908; becomes head of Reconstruction Finance Corporation, **12**-946

Dawes, William: warns Minutemen, **2**-122

Dawes Severalty Act: Congressional plan for Indians, **9**-665

Dayton, William L.: **6**-437

Dean, General William F.: **15**-1181

Dearborn, Henry: in War of 1812, **4**-275, 278, 283

Death March: on Bataan, **14**-1071

Debs, Eugene V.: in Pullman strike, **9**-690; imprisoned, **11**-845; nominated for fifth time in 1920 election, **11**-869, 871

Decatur, Lieutenant Stephen: **3**-216, 230; **4**-250, 279, 293

Declaration of Independence: **2**-132

Declaration of United Nations: **14**-1070

Declaratory Act: **2**-109, 110

De Forest, Lee: radio pioneer, **10**-781

De Gaulle, Charles: leads Free French, **14**-1049, 1052; and liberation of Paris, **14**-1099; confers with Eisenhower, **16**-1225; and Summit meetings, **16**-1228

DeKalb, Baron Johann: **2**-140

Delaware, Lord Thomas West: 1-44

Demarcation, Line of: 1-16

Democratic Party: origin, **5**-328, 329

Democratic-Republicans: early political party, **3**-213; gain strength, **3**-218; in 1808 election, **4**-264; and United States Bank, **4**-269; in 1816 election, **4**-295; in 1820 election, **4**-304; in 1824 election, **4**-309

Dempsey, Jack: boxing champion, **11**-860; **12**-915, 936

Denmark: sells Virgin Islands to United States, **11**-827; attacked by Germany, **14**-1050

Dennis, Lawrence: fascist leader, **13**-1007

Dependent Pension Act: **9**-666, 676

Deposit Act: **5**-354

Depression: in agriculture, **12**-930, 931; spreads after stock market crash of 1929, **12**-933; attempts by Hoover to alleviate, **12**-939; deepens as Hoover administration ends: **12**-956; New Deal measures, **13**-970-1015

Dew, Thomas R.: **6**-416

Dewey, Commodore George: wins Battle of Manila Bay, **9**-700

Dewey, John: proposes new teaching methods, **11**-826; **13**-1027

Dewey, Thomas E.: in election of 1944, **14**-1100; in election of 1948, **15**-1153

Dias, Bartholomew: 1-11

Diaz, Porfirio: Mexican dictator, **10**-790

Dickens, Charles: tours America, **5**-370

Dickinson, John: **2**-125

Dies, Martin: **15**-1151

Dingley, Nelson R.: sponsors high tariff, **9**-696

Dinwiddie, Governor Robert: **2**-93

Displaced Persons Bill: allows admission of homeless war victims, **15**-1148

District of Columbia: **3**-195

Dix, Dorothea L.: attempts to improve conditions in insane

asylums, **5**-395

Dixie: popular Civil War song, **7**-502

"Dixiecrats": **15**-1152

Doheny, Edward L.: in Harding scandals, **12**-907

Dole, Sanford B.: heads Hawaiian republic, **9**-683

Dolfuss, Engelbert: assassinated, **13**-1020

Domestic Allotment Act: **13**-1004

Dominican Republic: **10**-752, 754; **11**-818

Doolittle, Colonel James H.: and bombing of Tokyo, **14**-1077

Dorr, Thomas W.: and rebellion to liberalize suffrage, **5**-372

Dos Passos, John: writer, **12**-935; **13**-1026

Douglas, Stephen A.: and Young Americans, **6**-417; and Compromise of 1850, **6**-426; and Kansas-Nebraska Act, **6**-427; in 1856 election, **6**-428, 437; debates with Lincoln, **6**-448-449; and popular sovereignty, **6**-461; background, **6**-469; in 1860 election, **6**-471; and Crittenden Compromise, **6**-473; death of, **7**-501

Douglass, Frederick: **6**-411

Drago, Luis: protests against forcible collection of debts, **10**-745

Drago Doctrine: **10**-745; revised, **10**-762

Drake, Edward L.: **6**-456

Drake, Sir Francis: 1-34, 35, 36, 38

Dudington, Lt. William: and Gaspee Incident, **2**-115

Dulles, John Foster: **15**-1178, 1196; **16**-1217

Dumbarton Oaks Conference: **14**-1098

Dunkirk: evacuation of, **14**-1051

Dutch: in America, 1-42, 50

Dutch East India Company: 1-50

Dutch West India Company: 1-50

E

Earhart, Amelia: first woman to cross Atlantic in airplane, **12**-923

Early, General Jubal: at Battle of Gettysburg, **7**-522; advances on Washington, **7**-536

East India Company: 1-32; **2**-117

Eaton, Frederick: **16**-1232

Eaton, William: **4**-250

Eaton Affair: divides Jackson's cabinet, **5**-335

Eckener, Doctor Hugo: **12**-925

Eden, Anthony: at Moscow Conference, **14**-1092; at Summit meeting, **15**-1187; and Suez crisis, **15**-1190

Ederle, Gertrude: first woman to swim English Channel, **12**-915

Edison, Thomas A.: background and early inventions, **8**-633; develops sound films, **10**-782

Education: in New England colonies, 1-49, 54; emphasized in early America, **2**-155; influence of Webster's dictionary, **4**-313; and reforms of Horace Mann,

5-362; appointment of Commissioner of Education, **8**-581; elective system of Charles W. Eliot, **8**-596; fostered by Chatauqua movement, **9**-716; aided by philanthropists, **10**-729, 737, 739; and progressive ideas by John Dewey, **11**-826; **13**-1027; in the 1020's, **12**-935; aided by N.Y.A. program, **13**-997; and ideas of Robert M. Hutchins, **13**-1027; and G.I. Bill of Rights, **14**-1097; creation of Department of Health, Education and Welfare, **15**-1180; National Defense Education Act, **16**-1218

Edwards, Jonathan: early colonial preacher, **2**-91

Egypt: in World War II, **14**-1080; Cairo conferences, **14**-1093; and Suez crisis, **15**-1190; Nasser becomes president, **16**-1208

Einstein, Albert: wins Nobel Prize for Physics, **12**-900; warns Roosevelt on atomic weapons, **13**-1029

Eisenhower, General Dwight D.: commands North African invasion, **14**-1082; named commander, **14**-1086; and invasion of Sicily, **14**-1090; chosen to head European invasion, **14**-1093; and D-Day, **14**-1096; in liberation of Paris, **14**-1099; named Supreme Commander of NATO forces, **15**-1167; nominated for President, **15**-1176; elected in 1952, **15**-1177; studies Korean situation, **15**-1177; and China question, **15**-1178; urges peaceful use of atomic energy, **15**-1183; suffers heart attack, **15**-1186; at Summit meeting, **15**-1187; and Suez crisis, **15**-1190; and "Atoms for Peace" plan, **15**-1193; renominated with Vice-President Richard M. Nixon against Stevenson and Kefauver, **15**-1194; reelected, **15**-1195; bolsters hopes for peace, **15**-1196; and crisis in Lebanon, **16**-1215; acts in shelling of Chinese Nationalist islands, **16**-1217; comments on St. Lawrence Seaway, **16**-1221; on Hawaiian statehood, **16**-1222; confers with Khrushchev, **16**-1223; visits eleven nations, **16**-1225; and U-2 incident, **16**-1227; and Summit meeting, **16**-1228; breaks relations with Cuba, **16**-1239

Eisenhower Doctrine: **16**-1215, 1216

Elections: of 1789, **3**-184; of 1792, **3**-204; of 1796, **3**-213; of 1800, **3**-225; of 1804, **4**-254; of 1808, **4**-264; of 1812, **4**-274; of 1816, **4**-295; of 1820, **4**-304; of 1824, **4**-309; of 1828, **4**-315; of 1832, **5**-340; of 1836, **5**-357; of 1840, **5**-365; of 1844, **5**-379; of 1848, **5**-390; of 1852, **6**-422; of 1856, **6**-437; of 1860, **6**-471; of 1864, **7**-540; of 1868, **8**-591; of 1872, **8**-607; of 1876, **8**-624-625; of

E (contd.)

1880, **8**-635; of 1884, **9**-658; of 1888, **9**-667; of 1892, **9**-682; of 1896, **9**-693; of 1900, **9**-714; of 1904, **10**-751; of 1908, **10**-766; of 1912, **10**-780; of 1916, **11**-825; of 1920, **11**-869, 871; of 1924, **12**-908; of 1928, **12**-926; of 1932, **12**-955; of 1936, **13**-1009; of 1940, **14**-1060; of 1944, **14**-1100; of 1948, **15**-1152; of 1952, **15**-1177; of 1956, **15**-1195; of 1960, **16**-1230; of 1962, **16**-1246; of 1964, **16**-1256

Electoral College: 3-184

Eliot, Charles William: named president of Harvard University, **8**-596

Eliot, T. S.: poet, **12**-935

Elizabeth I, Queen of England: builds English power, **1**-32, 34; and Sir Walter Raleigh, **1**-36; war with Spain, **1**-38

Elizabeth II, Queen of England: dedicates St. Lawrence Seaway, **16**-1221

Elkins Act: 10-746

Emancipation Proclamation: issued by Lincoln, **7**-518

Embargo Act: under Jefferson, **4**-261, 262

Emergency Relief Appropriations Act, 13-1019

Emerson, Dr. John: 6-440

Emerson, Ralph Waldo: American writer, **7**-544

Emigrant aid societies: settle in West, **6**-426; form Free State Party, **6**-431

Empress of China: first American vessel at Canton, China, **3**-171

England: see Great Britain

Entente Cordiale: 10-756

Era of Good Feeling: under Monroe, **4**-295

Erie Canal: 4-310

Erskine, David M.: 4-264

Esch-Cummins Act: returns railroads to private ownership, **11**-868

Ethiopia: invaded by Italy, **13**-1001

European Relief Council: 11-855

Eustis, William: 4-278

Evans, George H.: labor leader, **5**-330

Everett, Edward: 6-464

Ex parte Milligan decision: Supreme Court rules on writ of habeas corpus, **8**-579

Explorer I: U. S. satellite circles earth, **16**-1213

F

Fair Deal: launched by Truman, **15**-1154

Fair Labor Standards Act: establishes minimum wages and maximum hours, **13**-1023

Fall, Albert B.: in Harding Scandals, **12**-907

Fallen Timbers, Battle of: 3-206

Farm Credit Act: liberalizes farm loan policy, **13**-979

Farm Security Administration: 13-1014

Farragut, Rear Admiral David G.: 7-508, 538

Father Divine: religious leader, **13**-1027

Faubus, Orval M.: and Little Rock integration issue, **16**-1211

Faure Edgar: 15-1187

Federal Communications Commission: established, **13**-991

Federal Courts: jurisdiction of, **3**-190

Federal Deposit Insurance Corporation: guarantees bank deposits, **13**-970

Federal Emergency Relief Administration, 13-973

Federal Farm Board: 12-931

Federal Farm Loan Act: 11-822

Federal Home Loan Bank Act: 12-951

Federal Housing Administration: 13-993

Federalists: early political party, **3**-213; and immigration, **3**-218; in 1804 election, **4**-254; in 1808 election, **4**-264; and United States Bank, **4**-269; and Hartford Convention, **4**-291; in 1820 election, **4**-304

Federal Reserve System: 10-789

Federal Trade Commission: 10-795; **13**-1022

Field, Cyrus: and Atlantic Cable, **6**-447, **8**-581

Fillmore, Millard: elected Vice-President, **5**-390; becomes President, **6**-413; and American Party, **6**-464

Finland: pays World War I debts, **13**-1033; invaded by Russia, **13**-1033; fights on Axis side, **14**-1064

Finlay, Doctor Carlos J.: fights against yellow fever, **9**-713

First Continental Congress: 2-119

Fish, Hamilton: negotiates Washington Treaty, **8**-602; negotiates Virginius settlement, **8**-612

Fisk, James: and gold plot, **8**-595

Fitch, John: 3-182

Fitzgerald, F. Scott: writer, **12**-935

Fitzhugh, George: 6-443

Fletcher versus Peck: Supreme Court decision in land question, **4**-268

Florida: early explorations, **1**-20, 29, 33; ceded to United States, **4**-301; in real estate boom, **12**-912

Foch, Marshal Ferdinand: named commander of Western Front, **11**-846; in armistice negotiations, **11**-854

Fong, Hiram L.: 16-1222

Foraker Act: establishes government for Puerto Rico, **9**-711, **10**-732

Forbes, Colonel Charles R.: in Harding scandals, **12**-906

Force Act: in Rhode Island, **3**-175

Force Bill: used in enforcement of revenue laws, **5**-342

Ford, Edsel: 12-921

Ford, Henry: and mass production of autos, **10**-769; and Peace Ship, **11**-816; and growth of company, **12**-921

Fordney-McCumber Tariff: 12-897

Forest Reserve Act: 10-741

Formosa: becomes headquarters of Chinese Nationalists, **15**-1159; blockade lifted, **15**-1178; and mutual defense pact, **15**-1185; and United States protection, **16**-1217

Forrestal, James V.: 15-1141

Fort Dearborn Massacre: 4-276

Fort Donelson: 7-503

Fort Duquesne: 2-94, 97

Fort Erie: 4-286

Fort Henry: 7-503

Fort Necessity: 2-94

Fort Pitt: 2-97, 103

Fort Sumter: fired upon, **6**-475

Forty-Niners: 5-392

Fountain of Youth: 1-20

Four Freedoms: 14-1061

Fourteen Points: summary of Wilson's program for peace, **11**-844; considered at Paris peace conference, **11**-856

France: and explorations of Verrazano, **1**-25; sends Cartier to North America, **1**-28; in early Florida, **1**-33; in Canada, **1**-40; and New World goals, **1**-43; and voyages of Joliet and Marquette, **1**-62; opposed by Iroquois, **1**-63; and explorations of La Salle, **1**-68; sends workers to New World, **1**-75; fights England in King George's War, **2**-92; rejects Washington's request to leave Ohio Valley, **2**-93; in French and Indian War, **2**-94, 96-101; joins Americans in war against British, **2**-145; sends Genet to America, **3**-201; and XYZ affair, **3**-214; in undeclared war with United States, **3**-216; in Santo Domingo, **3**-234; and effect of Napoleonic wars on America, **4**-255; and American neutral rights, **4**-260, 261, 267; contemplates intervention in Latin America, **4**-306; settles claims of United States, **5**-338; sends Tocqueville, **5**-347; establishes monarchy in Mexico, **7**-531; and fall of Maximilian, **8**-584; and gift of Statue of Liberty, **9**-662; in North African rivalries, **10**-756; and start of World War I, **10**-793, **11**-808-809; and American action in World War I, **11**-840, 841, 846-852; considers peace terms, **11**-854; at Washington Conference, **12**-895; occupies Ruhr, **12**-903; at London Naval Conference, **12**-937; and reparations moratorium, **12**-944; declares war on Germany, **13**-1031; fall of, **14**-1052; and Allied invasion, **14**-1096; becomes permanent member of Security Council, **15**-1130; signs Brussels Pact, **15**-1145; and Indo-China, **15**-1182; in Summit Conference of 1955, **15**-1187; and Summit conference, **16**-1228; protests Berlin Wall, **16**-1240

Franco, Francisco: in Spanish civil war, **13**-1005; becomes dictator of Spain, **13**-1011

Franklin, Benjamin: drafts Albany Plan of Union, **2**-95; and Declaration of Independence, **2**-132; heads delegation to France, **2**-145; and commission to England, **2**-154; at Constitutional Convention, **3**-177

Franklin, Battle of: 7-545

Fredericksburg, Battle of: 7-516

Freedmen's Bureau: established, **7**-548; continued by Congress, **8**-573

Freedom of the Press: 2-90

Freedom 7: Mercury space capsule, **16**-1237

Freedom March: on Washington, **16**-1249

Freeport Doctrine: 6-449

Free Soil Party: anti-slavery coalition, **5**-390; and 1852 election, **6**-419

Free State Party: 6-431

Frelinghuysen, Frederick T.: 9-652

Fremont, John C.: charts frontier areas, **5**-373; in Mexican War, **5**-386; in election of 1856, **6**-437; in election of 1864, **7**-534

French and Indian War: 2-93-99, 101

French Panama Canal Company: negotiates to sell canal rights, **10**-742, 748

Freneau, Philip: early American poet, **1**-72

Frick, Henry C.: 9-681; **11**-862

Friendship 7: Mercury space capsule orbits earth three times, **16**-1241

Fries, John: rebels against federal property tax, **3**-220

Frondizi, Arturo: 16-1214

Fugitive Slave Act: increases sectional bitterness, **6**-408-410; and Republican Party, **6**-428; and Davis resolutions, **6**-459; and Crittenden Compromise, **6**-473

Fulton, Robert: builds steamboat Clermont, **4**-258

Fundamental Orders of Connecticut: first formal constitution, **1**-57

G

Gadsden Purchase: 6-424

Gagarin, Major Yuri: 16-1235

Gage, General Thomas: 2-121, 123

Gag Rule: suppresses abolitionist petitions, **5**-357

Gallatin, Albert: appointed Secretary of the Treasury, **3**-229; favors Bank of the United States, **4**-269; as peace commissioner, **4**-284

Gama, Vasco da: 1-17

Gardoqui, Don Diego de: 3-174

Garfield, James A.: in 1880 Republican convention, **8**-634; elected President, **8**-635; restores executive power, **9**-650; assassinated, **9**-651

Garrison, William Lloyd: edits The Liberator, **5**-336; and abolitionist activity, **5**-349

Gaspee Incident: 2-115

G (contd.)

Gates, General Horatio: 2·142, 150

Geary, John W.: 6·436

Geary Act: excludes Chinese immigrants, 9·680

General Accounting Office: 12·890

Genet, Edmond: represents new French republic, 3·201

Geneva Naval Conference (1927): fails to achieve aims, 12·918

"Gentlemen's Agreement": limits Japanese immigration, 10·764

George II, King of England: 1·74, 2·96

George III, King of England: negotiates with French, 2·99; issues Proclamation of 1763, 2·102; adopts tax program, 2·108; declares colonies in rebellion, 2·127; receives John Adams, 3·173

George, Lloyd: announces Great Britain's war aims, 11·844; at Paris peace conference, 11·856

Georgia: founded, 1·74; and Sherman's march to the sea, 7·542-543

German Democratic Republic: created under Russian auspices, 15·1157

German Federal Republic: sponsored by Western Allies, 15·1157, 1170; as subject of Summit meeting, 15·1187

Germantown, Battle of: 2·141

Germany: in Samoan question, 9·671, 707; in Venezuelan debt dispute, 10·744, 745; and causes of World War I, 11·808-809; and sinking of Lusitania, 11·812-813; resumes submarine attacks, 11·829; and Zimmermann note, 11·832; at war with United States (1917), 11·835-854; signs treaty of Versailles, 11·861; and official end of war with United States, 12·891; in war debts and reparations questions, 12·903, 929; and rise of Hitler, 13·972; reoccupies Rhineland, 13·1001; becomes Axis partner, 13·1005; aids Franco, 13·1011; annexes Austria, 13·1020; and Hitler's appeasement at Munich, 13·1024; seizes Czechoslovakia, 13·1028; signs pact with Soviet Union, 13·1030; attacks Poland, 13·1031; launches "blitzkrieg" in Europe, 14·1050, 1051; defeats France, 14·1052; in Battle of Britain, 14·1055; attacks Russia 14·1064; defeated in North Africa, 14·1086; defeated at Salingrad, 14·1087; defeated in Western Europe, 14·1096, 1099, 1101; surrenders, 14·1110; occupation of discussed at Posdam, 14·1113; and occupation problems, 15·1143; and Berlin Blockade, 15·1147; and East-West split, 15·1157; continues as Cold War problem, 16·1240

Gerry, Elbridge: in XYZ Affair, 3·214;

elected Vice-President, 4·274

Gershwin, George: modern composer, 12·935

Gettysburg Address: 7·525

Gettysburg, Battle of: 7·521-522

Giddings, Joshua R.: 5·369

Gilbert Islands: 14·1095

Giraud, General Henri: 14·1083

Glass-Owen Act: creates Federal Reserve System, 10·789

Glass-Steagall Act: attempts to stimulate economy, 12·947

Glavis, Louis R.: 10·772, 773

Glenn, Lt. Col. John H.: becomes first American to orbit earth, 16·1241

Godfrey, Thomas: playwright, 2·106

Goethals, Colonel George W.: and construction of Panama Canal, 10·760

Gold: discovered in California, 5·391-392; and effects on law enforcement, 6·412; stimulates travel, 6·429; found in Colorado, 6·452; in Nevada, 6·453; in Klondike, 9·694

Gold Question: affected by silver purchases, 9·675; in Panic of 1893, 9·685; falling reserves cause crisis, 9·687; purchases from bankers bolster economy, 9·692; in campaigns of 1896, 9·693; supply increases, 9·696; gold standard adopted, 9·710; gold standard abandoned, 13·985

Goldberg, Arthur J.: appointed as U.N. Ambassador, 16·1260

Goldwater, Barry: defeated in 1964 presidential election, 16·1256

Gompers, Samuel: becomes president of American Federation of Labor, 9·663; death of, 12·910

Gomulka, Wladyslaw: 15·1192

Good Neighbor Policy: 12·928, 13·984

Goodyear, Charles: discovers vulcanizing process, 5·377

Gore, Thomas P.: 11·821

Gorgas, Major William C.: fights yellow fever in Cuba, 10·730; in Panama, 10·760

Gorky, Maxim: seeks aid for starving Russians, 12·893

Gospel of Wealth: reveals Carnegie's philosophy, 10·737

Gould, Jay: and gold plot of 1869, 8·595

Graf Zeppelin: 12·925

Graham, William A.: 6·418

Grand Army of the Republic: and Confederate flag controversy, 9·666; dispute with Cleveland over pensions, 9·666, 667

Grange, Harold (Red): football hero of the 1920's, 12·936

Grange: created to aid farmers, 8·585; attacks railroad abuses, 9·664

Granger, Gideon: first Postmaster General, 4·266

Grant, Ulysses S.: background and role in Western Campaign, 7·503;

at Battle of Shiloh, 7·506; at siege of Vicksburg, 7·523; named commander in West, 7·527; given command of all Union armies, 7·530; in Wilderness Campaign, 7·532; and surrender of Lee, 7·550; orders troops to Mexican border, 8·574; elected President, 8·591; reelected, 8·607; scandals in administration, 8·595, 603, 606, 609, 616, 618, 636; death of, 9·659

Gravelet, Jean Francois: see Blondin, The Great

Gray, Robert: sails around the world, 3·193; explores Columbia River, 3·199

Great Awakening: religious revival, 2·91

Great Britain: in North American explorations, 1·18; and foundations of empire, 1·32; defeats Spanish Armada, 1·38; founds Jamestown, 1·39, 44-46; and Massachusetts Colony, 1·47-49; and Massachusetts Bay, 1·51-52; and grant to Lord Baltimore of Maryland, 1·53; grants charter for Rhode Island, 1·55; and Connecticut colony, 1·57; and New England Confederation, 1·58; takes New Netherlands from Dutch, 1·61; and grant to William Penn of Pennsylvania, 1·67; and founding of Georgia, 1·74; criticized by Zenger, 2·90; in King George's War, 2·92; in French and Indian War, 2·93-101; and Proclamation Line of 1763, 2·102; acts in Pontiac's Rebellion, 2·103; imposes stamp tax, 2·108-109; and Townshend Acts, 2·110-111; and Boston Massacre, 2·113; and Gaspee incident, 2·115; passes Tea Act, 2·117; and Boston Tea Party, 2·117; imposes Intolerable Acts, 2·118; and Revolutionary War, 2·122-153; signs Treaty of Paris giving Americans independence, 2·154; in war with France, 3·201, 207, 208; and American neutral rights, 4·255, 257, 260, 265, 267, 270, 273; in the War of 1812, 4·275-292; and Rush-Bagot agreement, 4·297; and Caroline affair, 5·361; and Webster-Ashburton Treaty, 5·374; and dispute over Oregon, 5·383; in Honduran Bay "Mosquito War," 6·429; recognizes South as belligerent in Civil War, 7·495; and involvement with Confederate envoys, 7·500; and Samoa, 9·671, 707; and Bering Sea sealing controversy, 9·686; and Venezuelan boundary question, 9·709; in Venezuelan debt question, 10·744, 745; in Alaskan boundary dispute, 10·747; joins France in Entente Cordiale, 10·756; and causes of World War I, 11·808-809; defends blockade, 11·813; at Washington

Conference, 12·895; at Geneva Naval Conference, 12·918; in 1929 economic crisis, 12·933; at London Naval Conference, 12·937; and breakdown of negotiations with Soviet Union, 13·1030; declares war on Germany, 13·1031; and Dunkirk evacuation, 14·1051; in Battle of Britain, 14·1055; in African Campaign, 14·1080; becomes permanent member of Security Council, 15·1130; and German question, 15·1143; signs Brussels Pact, 15·1145; withdraws from Palestine, 15·1146; and NATO, 15·1155; in atoms for peace program, 15·1183; and Suez crisis, 15·1190; in Lebanon crisis, 16·1215; and Summit conference, 16·1228; protests Berlin Wall, 16·1240

Great Treaty of Pennsylvania: 1·67

Greece: invaded by Axis, 14·1059; and Communist question, 15·1130; receives aid, 15·1135, 1137

Greeley, Horace: editor and publisher, 5·368; writes "Prayer of Twenty Millions," 7·514; in election of 1872, 8·605, 607

Greenback Labor Party: success in Congressional elections of 1878, 8·629; declines in election of 1880, 8·635

Greenback Party: in election of 1876, 8·622

Greene, John: 3·171

Greene, General Nathaniel: 2·150

Greenland: occupied by American troops, 14·1063

Green Mountain Boys: 2·124, 141

Greenville, Peace of: 3·206

Grenville, George: imposes Quartering and Stamp Acts, 2·108

Grenville, Sir Richard: 1·36

Grey, Sir Edward: 11·819

Grimke, Angelina: 6·411

Grimke, Sarah: 6·411

Grissom, Captain Virgil I.: makes second U.S. sub-orbital flight, 16·1238

Gruening, Ernest: 16·1222

Grundy, Felix: 4·271

Guadalcanal: 14·1081

Guadalupe-Hidalgo, Treaty of: ends Mexican War, 5·389

Guam: ceded to United States, 9·705

Guiteau, Charles G.: assassinates President Garfield, 9·651

H

Haile Selassie: 13·1001

Haiti: discovered by Columbus, 1·15; and "dollar diplomacy," 11·818; and United States Good Neighbor Policy, 13·984

Hale, John R.: 6·422

Hale, Nathan: 2·136

"Half-Breeds": Republican Party faction, 9·650

Halleck, General Henry W.:

H (contd.)

commands Union Army in the West, **7**-503; at Corinth and Memphis, **7**-508; becomes general-in-chief of Union forces, **7**-513

Halsey, Admiral William F. Jr.: **14**-1102

Hamilton, Alexander: favors new constitution, **3**-176; at Constitutional Convention, **3**-177; and Federalist Papers, **3**-180; named Secretary of the Treasury, **3**-186; plans to restore America's credit, **3**-187; proposes United States Bank, **3**-194; and assumption of state debts, **3**-195; favors strong central government, **3**-204; role in election of 1800, **3**-226; killed in duel with Aaron Burr, **4**-253

Hamilton, Andrew: defends Peter Zenger, **2**-90

Hamilton, Colonel Henry: **2**-146

Hamlin, Hannibal, **6**-465

Hammarskjold, Dag: and crisis in Middle East, **16**-1215

Hammond, Henry: Southern writer, **6**-443

Hampton, General Wade: **4**-283

Hancock, John: and Liberty Incident, **2**-111; President of Second Continental Congress, **2**-125; signs Declaration of Independence, **2**-132

Hancock, General Winfield S.: at Battle of Gettysburg, **7**-522; as Presidential candidate, **8**-634

Hanna, Marcus ("Mark"): manages McKinley's campaign, **9**-695

Harding, Warren G.: nominated for President, **11**-869; wins in election of 1920, **11**-871; and Washington Conference, **12**-894; death of, **12**-898; and corruption in administration, **12**-906-907

Harmer, General Josiah: **3**-198

Harper, William: **6**-416

Harper's Ferry: and raid of John Brown, **6**-457

Harris, Townsend: and Japanese relations, **6**-425, 445, 462

Harrison, Benjamin: elected President, **9**-667; and policies, **9**-676; loses in 1892, **9**-682

Harrison, William Henry: at Tippecanoe, **4**-272; in War of 1812, **4**-281, 282; elected President, **5**-365; death of **5**-367

Hartford Convention: proposes revisions to Constitution, **4**-291

Harvard, John: **1**-56

Harvard College: founded, **1**-56

Hauptmann, Bruno: **12**-948

Havana, Cuba: in yellow fever campaign, **10**-730, occupied by Castro's army, **16**-1220

Havana, Act of: **14**-1054

Hawaii: recognized as republic, **9**-683; annexed, **9**-703; and establishment of government, **9**-711; admitted as state, **16**-1222

Hawkins, Samuel: **3**-192

Hawley Smoot Tariff: **12**-938

Hay, John: and Open Door notes, **9**-708, 712; in Roosevelt cabinet, **10**-735; and Panama Canal, **10**-742, 748

Hay-Bunau-Varilla Treaty: **10**-748

Hay-Pauncefote Treaty: **10**-736

Hayes, Rutherford B.: nominated for President, **8**-622; wins disputed election of 1876, **8**-625; uses Federal troops in railroad strike, **8**-627; opposes spoils system and defends civil service, **8**-632; refuses to run for reelection, **8**-634

Haymarket Riot: and strike violence, **9**-660

Hayne, Robert Y.: advocates states' rights, **5**-331; carries on fight for nullification, **5**-342

Health, Education and Welfare, Department of: created, **15**-1180

Hearst, William Randolph: **9**-697

Helper, Hinton: **6**-442

Hemingway, Ernest: writer, **12**-935; **13**-1026

Henderson, Leon: **14**-1075

Hendricks, Thomas A.: **9**-659

Henry, Patrick: attacks English abuses, **2**-108, 116, 121

Henry VII, King of England: **1**-13, 19

Henry the Navigator, Prince: **1**-10

Herkimer, General Nicholas: at Battle of Oriskany, **2**-141

Hillman, Sidney: labor leader, and a founder of the CIO, **13**-1025

Hindenburg, Paul von: and German submarine warfare, **11**-829; names Hitler as Chancellor, **13**-972

Hindenburg disaster: dirigible explosion, **13**-1012

Hirohito, Emperor of Japan: becomes national symbol, **14**-1049; retains throne, **14**-1115

Hiroshima: **14**-1114

Hiss, Alger: **15**-1151

Hitler, Adolf: also see Germany; becomes German leader, **13**-972; reoccupies Rhineland, **13**-1001; and Rome-Berlin Axis, **13**-1005; annexes Austria, **13**-1020; seizes Sudetenland, **13**-1024; signs pact with Stalin, **13**-1030; invades Poland, **13**-1031; and aggressions, **14**-1048; attacks Soviet Union, **14**-1064; and African campaign, **14**-1086; in second Russian offensive, **14**-1087; rescues Mussolini, **14**-1091; and Battle of Bulge, **14**-1101; death of, **14**-1110

Hobby, Oveta Culp: head Women's Army Corps, **14**-1084; becomes Secretary of Health, Education and Welfare, **15**-1180

Hoffman, Paul: leads European Recovery Program after World War II, **15**-1138

Holmes, Oliver Wendell: **10**-753

Homestead Act: **7**-512

Homestead Strike: and violence

at Carnegie Steel Company, **9**-681

Homma, Masaharu: **15**-1145

Honduras: and "dollar diplomacy," **10**-776

Hood, General John B.: and defense of Atlanta, **7**-537; at Battle of Nashville, **7**-545

Hooker, General Joseph: named commander of Army of Potomac, **7**-516; resigns command, **7**-521

Hooker, Thomas: migrates to Connecticut, **1**-57

Hoover, Herbert: heads Food Administration, **11**-839; becomes Chairman of European Relief Council, **11**-855; and Russian aid, **12**-893; nominated for President, **12**-926; elected **12**-927; adopts Good Neighbor Policy, **12**-928; and confidence in American economy, **12**-932; and London Naval Conference, **12**-937; signs Hawley-Smoot Tariff, **12**-938; attacks depression, **12**-939; and Wickersham Commission, **12**-941; declares debt moratorium, **12**-944; and Manchurian incident, **12**-945; vetoes Wagner-Garner Bill, **12**-947; orders bonus marchers dispersed, **12**-950; and World Court, **12**-952; and Presidential Campaign of 1932, **12**-953-955; and commission to reorganize executive department, **15**-1156; and debate over Korean War, **15**-1167

Hoover Dam: **13**-1008

Hopkins, Harry: appointed Federal Relief Administrator, **13**-973; directs Civil Works Administration **13**-981; becomes head of Works Progress Administration, **13**-994

House, Edward M.: as Wilson's advisor, **10**-780; on peace missions to Europe, **11**-819; at Paris Peace Conference, **11**-856; advises Wilson to resign, **11**-863

House of Burgesses: and self-rule in Virginia, **1**-46; passes Virginia Resolves, **2**-108; holds revolutionary convention, **2**-121

Houston, General Sam: commands Texas army, **5**-351; defeats Santa Anna, **5**-353

Howe, Elias: invents sewing machine, **5**-385; sues Singer, **6**-420

Howe, Julia Ward: writes Battle Hymn of the Republic, **7**-502

Howe, General William: **2**-128, 131, 135, 141, 144

Hudson, Henry: explores Hudson River and Bay, **1**-42; searches for Northwest Passage, **1**-50

Hudson Bay Company: **4**-263

Huerta, Victoriano: establishes Mexican government, **10**-790-791

Hughes, Charles E.: in election of 1916, **11**-825; at Washington Conference, **12**-895; at Pan-American Conference, **12**-922; and World Court, **12**-952; and

Supreme Court, **13**-1010

Huguenots: **1**-33

Hull, Cordell: becomes Secretary of State, **13**-968; at London Economic Conference, **13**-977; supports Good Neighbor Policy, **13**-984; concludes reciprocal tariff agreements, **13**-989; at Moscow Conference, **14**-1092; rejects Japan's demands, **14**-1068; receives Japanese note after Pearl Harbor, **14**-1069

Hull, Captain Isaac: **4**-279

Hull, General William: **4**-275, 276

Hull House: social service center founded by Jane Addams, **9**-672

Hulsemann, Chevalier: **6**-414

Humphrey, Hubert H.: elected Vice-President in 1964, **16**-1256

Hungary: and revolutionary activities of Kossuth, **6**-414; joins Axis, **14**-1059; becomes Soviet satellite, **15**-1144; revolts against Russians, **15**-1192

Hunt, Walter: **6**-420

Huron Indians: **1**-40

Hussein, King of Jordan: **16**-1215

Hutchins, Robert Maynard: American educator, **13**-1027

Hutchinson, Anne: at Providence, **1**-55

Hydrogen bomb: first explosion by United States, **15**-1175; exploded by Russia, **15**-1183; "fallout" peril, **15**-1183

I

Iceland: occupied by American forces, **14**-1063

Ickes, Harold L.: becomes head of Public Works Administration, **13**-978

Idaho: admitted as state, **9**-668

Immigration: attracts European workers to America, **5**-375; reaction against, **6**-417; and restrictions, **11**-830, **12**-905

Impeachment: first use of, **3**-215; of Chase and Pickering, **4**-252; of President Johnson, **8**-586-587

Impressment: of American seamen, **4**-255; increase in, **4**-270

Incas: **1**-27

Income Tax: helps North finance Civil War, **7**-535; legalized by Sixteenth Amendment, **10**-783, 788

Indentured servants: **1**-45

Independent Treasury Act: passed, **5**-359; repealed, **5**-367

Indians: in New France, **1**-40; and John Smith, **1**-41; early activities of, **1**-63-65; in Northwest Territory, **3**-198; and Andrew Jackson, **4**-285; and removal by Jackson, **5**-339; and effects of Colt revolver, **5**-348; massacre Whitman's band, **5**-388; Indian wars and reservations, **8**-614-615; Custer massacre, **8**-623; Dawes Act, **9**-665; citizenship, **13**-990

Indo-China: **15**-1182

Industry: aided by interchangeable parts, **3**-228; encouraged by

I (contd.)

tariffs, **4**·308; and development of farm machinery, **5**·345; and discovery of rubber process, **5**·377; and introduction of sewing machine, **6**·420; and steel-making, **6**·433; and discovery of oil, **6**·456; in North during Civil War, **7**·489; and transcontinental railroad, **8**·594; on display in Philadelphia Centennial, **8**·621; and activites of Rockefeller, **8**·631, **9**·653; and era of bridge building, **9**·655; and Interstate Commerce Act, **9**·664; creates monopolies, **9**·675, 679; and Andrew Carnegie, **10**·737; and Henry Ford, **10**·769; regulated by anti-trust laws, **10**·796; unites in World War I, **11**·839; and crash of 1929, **12**·933; aided by Reconstruction Finance Corporation, **12**·946; and effects of Tennessee Valley Authority, **13**·975; and National Industrial Recovery Act, **13**·978, 996; and controls of Federal Trade Commission, **13**·1022; enters era of prosperity, **13**·1036; unites in World War II, **14**·1072-1073, 1088

Industrial Workers of the World (I.W.W.): radical labor organization, **11**·823

Influenza: takes heavy toll in epidemic of 1918, **11**·853

Ingersoll, Charles: **4**·274

Inonu, Ismet: **14**·1093

Inouye, Daniel K.: **16**·1222

Insular Cases: **10**·732

International Atomic Energy Agency **15**·1193

International Conference of American States: sixth meeting at Havana (1928), **12**·922

International Geophysical Year: **16**·1212, 1219

Interstate Commerce Act: provides for regulatory commission, **9**·664; powers limited, **10**·746

Iran: protests occupation by Russia, **15**·1130; joins Baghdad Pact, **15**·1188

Iredell, James: **3**·220

Iroquois Indians: **1**·40, 63

Isabella, Queen of Spain: and Columbus, **1**·13, 14, 15

Island Number Ten: taken by Union troops, **7**·507

Israel: created and wars with Arabs, **15**·1146; and Suez crisis, **15**·1190

Italian trade monopolies: **1**·8

Italy: and causes of World War I, **11**·809; defeated at Caporetto, **11**·841; at Washington Conference, **12**·895; at London Naval Conference, **12**·937; invades Ethiopia, **13**·1001; becomes Axis partner, **13**·1005; in Spanish civil war, **13**·1011; attacks Albania, **13**·1028; attacks France, **14**·1052; defeated at Taranto, **14**·1059; defeated in

North Africa, **14**·1086; invaded by Allies, **14**·1090; surrenders, **14**·1091; peace treaty, **15**·1136

Iwo Jima, Battle of: **14**·1105

J

Jackson, Andrew: and Creek Indians, **4**·285; in Battle of New Orleans, **4**·292; and Seminole War, **4**·299; in 1824 election, **4**·309; elected President, **4**·315; administration begins, **5**·328-329; on federal supremacy, **5**·332; on federal aid, **5**·333; in Eaton affair, **5**·335; and shirtsleeve diplomacy, **5**·338; and Indian policy, **5**·339; reelected, **5**·340; threatens force in South Carolina, **5**·342; feuds with Biddle over Bank of United States, **5**·343; attempts to purchase Texas, **5**·351; issues Specie Circular, **5**·354

Jackson, Robert H.: **15**·1143

Jackson, General Thomas J. (Stonewall): at First Battle of Bull Run, **7**·497; in Peninsula Campaign, **7**·510; at Second Battle of Bull Run, **7**·513; death of, **7**·519

James I, King of England: grants charter to London Company, **1**·39; creates royal colony in Jamestown, **1**·46; and Separatists, **1**·47

James II, King of England: gives Penn land in America, **1**·67

Jamestown Colony: settled, **1**·39; under John Smith, **1**·41; women in, **1**·44; and first Negro workers, **1**·45; government of, **1**·46; burning of, **1**·66

Japan: opened by Perry, **6**·425; and commercial treaty, **6**·445; sends mission to America, **6**·462; in war with Russia, **10**·755; and immigration question, **10**·764; pressures China, **11**·842; and Lansing-Ishii agreement, **11**·842; assumes aggressive role in Pacific area, **12**·894; at Washington Conference, **12**·895; and violation of Gentlemen's Agreement, **12**·905; at Geneva Naval Conference, **12**·918; at London Naval Conference, **12**·937; and record of difficulties with United States, **12**·942; seizes Manchuria, **12**·943; condemned by League of Nations, **12**·945; attacks Shanghai, **12**·945; joins Axis, **13**·1005; attacks North China, **13**·1013; sinks Panay, **13**·1017; and aggressions in Southeast Asia, **14**·1058; and "peace" mission, **14**·1068; attacks Pearl Harbor, **14**·1069; early successes in World War II, **14**·1071, 1076; the tide turns, **14**·1078, 1079, 1081, 1094, 1095, 1102, 1103, 1105, 1106, 1107; given ultimatum, **14**·1113; hit by atomic bombs, **14**·1114;

surrenders, **14**·1115; occupation of, **15**·1145; regains sovereignty, **15**·1173

Java Sea, Battle of: **14**·1076

Jay, John: negotiates peace treaty with England, **2**·154; as minister to England, **3**·173; negotiates with Spain, **3**·174; named Chief Justice, **3**·186; and unpopular settlement with England, **3**·208

Jay's Treaty: **3**·208

Jazz: as modern musical form, **12**·935

Jefferson, Thomas: forms Committee of Correspondence, **2**·116; at Second Continental Congress, **2**·125; drafts Declaration of Independence, **2**·132; background of, **2**·133; suggests plan for Northwest Territory, **3**·172; as minister to France, **3**·173, named Secretary of State, **3**·186; opposes Bank of United States, **3**·194; favors southern capital, **3**·195; opposes Hamilton's program, **3**·204; and cession of state lands to United States, **3**·209; elected Vice-President, **3**·213; drafts Kentucky resolutions, **3**·219; elected President, **3**·225; inaugurated, **3**·229; Louisiana Purchase **3**·235; orders Lewis and Clark expedition, **4**·251; reelected, **4**·254; seeks treaty with England, **4**·255; warns British warships to leave, **4**·257; and embargo, **4**·261; signs Non-Intercourse Act, **4**·262; death of, **4**·311

Jeffries, Dr. John: **3**·200

Jenkins, John: **6**·412

John II, King of Portugal: **1**·13

Johnson, Andrew: elected Vice-President, **7**·540; assumes Presidency, **7**·551; and plan for reconstruction of South, **7**·554; feuds with Congress, **8**·577; dismisses Stanton and is impeached, **8**·586; acquitted by Senate, **8**·587; pardons Davis, **8**·592

Johnson, Herschel V.: **6**·468

Johnson, Hiram W.: opposes League, **11**·862

Johnson, Hugh S.: heads NRA, **13**·978

Johnson, Lyndon B.: elected **16**·1229; becomes President on assassination of Kennedy, **16**·1254; elected President in 1964, **16**·1256 **16**·1262

Johnson, Richard M.: War Hawk, **4**·271; and Battle of Thames, **4**·282

Johnson, Samuel: publishes dictionary, **4**·313

Johnson Debt Default Act: **13**·987

Johnson Immigration Act: **12**·905

Johnston, General Albert S.: killed at Battle of Shiloh, **7**·506

Johnston, General Joseph E.: at

Chickahominy, **7**·511; in battle for Atlanta, **7**·537; opposes Sherman in Carolinas, **7**·547; capitulates to Sherman, **7**·552

Johnstown, Pennsylvania: site of tragic flood, **9**·670

Joint Committee on the Conduct of the War: created, **7**·501; harasses Lincoln, **7**·517

Joint Congressional Committee on Reconstruction: submits Fourteenth Amendment, **8**·575

Joliet, Louis: explores Mississippi River, **1**·62

Jolson, Al: appears in first film carrying sound track, **12**·920

Jones, Bobby: golf champion, **11**·873

Jones, Captain Jacob: **4**·279

Jones, Captain John Paul: defeats British ship Serapis, **2**·148

Jones Act: for Philippine Islands, **11**·824; for Puerto Rico, **11**·833

Jordan: revolt in, **16**·1215

Juarez, Benito: opposes French in Mexico, **7**·531; and execution of Maximilian, **8**·584

Judicial review doctrine: asserts power of Supreme Court, **3**·231

Judiciary Act: of 1789, **3**·190; of 1801, **3**·231

Justice, Department of: created, **8**·601

K

Kadar, Janos: **15**·1192

Kansas: and slavery question, **6**·426, 431, 434, 435, 436, 438, 448; and temperance movement, **10**·731

Kansas-Nebraska Act: Stephen A. Douglas and slavery compromise, **6**·426, 427; and Republican Party, **6**·428; and Abraham Lincoln, **6**·444; and sectional strife, **6**·476

KDKA: pioneer radio broadcasting station, **11**·874

Kearney, Denis: **8**·628

Kearney, Colonel Stephen W.: in Mexican War, **5**·386

Kefauver, Estes: **15**·1171, 1194

Kellogg, Frank B.: and peace pact, **12**·924

Kellogg-Briand Pact: attempts to outlaw war, **12**·924; violated by Japan in Manchurian incident, **12**·943

Kelly, William: and development of steel process, **6**·433

Kelly Act: aids aviation, **12**·914

Kendrick, Captain John: **3**·193

Kennedy, John F.: debates with Nixon as Presidential nominee, **16**·1229; elected President, **16**·1230; background, **16**·1231; launches New Frontier Program, **16**·1234; Cuban invasion, **16**·1236; erection of Berlin Wall, **16**·1240; integration crisis, **16**·1243; blockades Cuba, **16**·1245; forces Soviet removal of missiles, **16**·1246; assassinated, **16**·1251;

K (contd.)

lies in state, 16-1252; funeral, 16-1253

Kennedy-Nixon TV debates: in 1960 election, 16-1235

Kentucky: explored by Daniel Boone, 2-112; becomes fifteenth state, 3-212

Key, Francis Scott: witnesses battle and writes Star Spangled Banner, 4-289

Khrushchev, Nikita: denounces Stalin, 15-1192; visits United States, 16-1223; and U-2 incident, 16-1227; breaks up Summit meeting 16-1228; commends Gagarin, 16-1235; and Cuban invasion, 16-1236; removes Soviet missiles from Cuba, 16-1246

Kidd, Captain William: 1-70

King, Martin Luther: 15-1191; 16-1257

King, Rufus: in 1804 election, 4-254; in 1808 election, 4-264; in 1816 election, 4-295

King, W. L. Mackenzie: 14-1056

King, William R.: 6-418, 422

King George's War: 2-92

King's Mountain, Battle of: 2-150

Kitchen cabinet: unofficial advisors to Jackson, 5-329

Klondike: gold rush, 9-694; boundary dispute, 9-694, 10-747

Knights of Labor: created, 8-597; call general strike, 9-660

Know-Nothing Party: secret society, 6-417; in 1852 election, 6-418, 419, 422

Knox, Frank: appointed Secretary of the Navy, 14-1053

Knox, General Henry: named Secretary of War, 3-186; sends troops to Northwest Territory, 3-198

Knox, Philander C.: as Attorney General, 10-750; Secretary of State, 10-776

Konoye, Prince Fuminaro: 14-1068

Korea: becomes center of postwar conflict, 15-1161; war in, 15-1162, 1163, 1165, 1167, 1172, 1177, 1181

Kosciusko, Thaddeus: aids Washington in American Revolution, 2-140

Kossuth, Louis: asks aid for Hungarian revolution, 6-414

Kuhn, Fritz: leads German-American Bund. 13-1007

Ku Klux Klan: Southern terrorist society, 8-599; re-emerges, 12-901

Kurusu, Saburo: 14-1068, 1069

Kwajalein: 14-1102

L

Labor: workers in New World, 1-75; and beginning of unions, 4-312; and organization of Workingmen's Party, 5-330; and formation of National Trades Union, 5-346; and

Jacksonians. 5-356: compared to slave workers, 6-443; gives advantage to North, 7-489; and National Labor Union, 8-576; formation of Knights of Labor, 8-597; and organization of American Federation of Labor, 9-663; objects to Chinese Workingmen, 9-680; and strikes of Colorado miners, 9-688; granted national holiday, 9-691; enters Twentieth Century, 10-728; and Roosevelt's Square Deal, 10-740; affected by Supreme Court decisions, 10-753, 763; given separate Cabinet office, 10-785; and anti-trust laws, 10-796; mobilizes in World War I, 11-843; and strikes of 1921, 12-892; and influence of Samuel Gompers, 12-910; and National Recovery Act, 13-978; and National Labor Relations Act, 13-998; and Fair Labor Standards Act, 13-1023; split by organization of CIO, 13-1025; in World War II, 14-1072; in postwar strikes, 15-1133; and Taft-Hartley Act, 15-1139; strike and government seizes steel industry, 15-1174; and Labor-Management Reporting and Disclosure Act, 16-1226

Lafayette, Marquis de: joins Washington in fight against British, 2-140; aids in capture of Cornwallis, 2-151

La Follette, Robert M.: leads Republican Progressives, 10-771; opposes League of Nations, 11-862; in election of 1924, 12-908

La Follette Seamen's Act: improves conditions of sailors, 11-811

LaGuardia, Fiorello: heads Office of Civilian Defense, 14-1075; directs UNRRA, 15-1135

Landon, Alfred M.: defeated in election of 1936, 13-1009

Lane, James: 6-431, 434

Lane, Joseph: 6-470

Lansing, Robert: appointed Secretary of State, 11-813; protests German submarine attacks, 11-814; and Santo Domingo intervention, 11-818; favors United States entry into war, 11-835; negotiates agreement with Japan, 11-842; accompanies Wilson to peace conference, 11-856

Lansing-Ishii Agreement: Japanese-American Far-Eastern accord, 11-842

La Salle, Robert Sieur de: travels Mississippi River, 1-68

Latin America: Monroe Doctrine, 4-307; Roosevelt Corollary, 10-752; Good Neighbor Policy, 12-928, 13-984; also see individual republics and conferences.

Latin American revolutions: 4-306

Latin School: 1-54, 56

Lattimore, Owen: 15-1160

Laurens, Henry: 2-154

Laval, Pierre: 14-1052

Lawrence, Captain James: 4-280

Lazear, Jesse W.: and yellow fever, 9-713

League of Nations: proposed in Wilson's Fourteen Points, 11-844; and drafting of Covenant, 11-858; presented to Senate, 11-861; defeated, 11-864; and election of 1920, 11-871; opens at Geneva, Switzerland, 11-875; ceases to be political issue, 12-891; and Manchurian incident, 12-943; condemns Japan, 12-945; adopts Stimson non-recognition policy, 12-945

Lebanon: revolt in, 16-1215

Ledyard, John: 3-171

Lee, General Henry: 3-205

Lee, Richard Henry: 2-132

Lee, General Robert E.: plans strategy against North's Peninsula Campaign, 7-510; takes command of Confederate Army of Northern Virginia and attacks at Mechanicsville, 7-511; launches invasion of the North, 7-515; at Battle of Gettysburg, 7-521, 522; in Wilderness Campaign, 7-532-533; becomes commander-in-chief of Confederate forces. 7-546; in final actions and surrender at Appomattox Courthouse, 7-550

L'Enfant, Major Pierre Charles: designs Washington, D.C., 3-195

Lehman, Herbert H.: 15-1135

Lend-Lease: 14-1062, 1063, 1116; 15-1149

Leon, Ponce de: 1-20

Lewis, John L.: leads coal miners in strikes, 11-865; 12-892; resigns from A. F. of L., 13-998; becomes head of CIO, 13-1025

Lewis, Meriwether: explores West, 4-251

Lewis, Sinclair: writer, 12-935

Lewis and Clark expedition: explores Far West, 4-251

Lexington, Battle of: 2-122, 123

Leyte Gulf, Battle of: 14-1103

Liberal Party: in election of 1844, 5-379

Liberator, The: first issue, 5-336; advocates abolition, 5-349

Liberty Bell: 2-132

Liberty Bell 7: Mercury space capsule in sub-orbital flight for U.S., 16-1244

Liberty Bonds: help finance World War I, 11-839

Library of Congress: founded, 3-224

Lie, Trygve H.: becomes first Secretary-General of U.N., 15-1130

Lilienthal, David E.: 13-975; 15-1132

Liliuokalani, Queen of Hawaii: dethroned in revolution, 9-683

Lincoln, Abraham: runs for Senate, 6-444; and debates with Douglas, 6-448-449; and Cooper-Union

speech, 6-461; in 1860 election, 6-465; background of, 6-444, 466-467; elected President, 6-471; rejects Crittenden Compromise, 6-473; at first inauguration, 7-491; sends aid to Fort Sumter, 7-492; issues call to arms, 7-493; proclaims blockade of South, 7-494; and strategy of war, 7-499; suspends writ of habeas corpus, 7-504; and Peninsular Campaign, 7-510; replies to Greeley, 7-514; issues Emancipation Proclamation, 7-518; delivers Gettysburg Address, 7-525; renominated, 7-534; plans reconstruction, 7-535, 549; reelected, 7-540; second inauguration, 7-549; assassination of, 7-551

Lincoln, General Benjamin: surrenders Charleston in Revolutionary War, 2-150; and Shays' Rebellion, 3-175

Lincoln, Robert T.: 9-652; 10-734

Lindbergh, Charles A.: makes first non-stop flight from New York to Paris, 12-916-917; and kidnapping of infant son, 12-948; leads isolationists, 13-1032

Line of Demarcation: 1-16

Little America: antarctic base of Byrd expedition, 12-934

Little Belt affair: 4-270

Little Rock, Arkansas: and school integration issue, 16-1211

Livingston, Robert: first United States Secretary of Foreign Affairs, 3-173; negotiates purchase of Louisiana Territory, 3-235

Lochner vs. New York: Supreme Court rules on labor laws, 10-753

Loco-Focos: radical wing of Democratic Party, 5-350

Locomotive: first use in America, 5-334

Lodge, Henry Cabot: and League of Nations controversy, 11-862, 864

Lodge, Henry Cabot: Vice-Presidential nominee in 1960 election, 16-1229

Lome, Dupuy de: 9-698

London Company: granted charter for Jamestown, 1-39; sends women, 1-44; grants Jamestown reform, 1-46

London Economic Conference: 13-977

London Naval Conference: 12-937

Long, Huey P.: and "Share-Our-Wealth Society," 13-1007

Longstreet, General James: at Second Battle of Bull Run, 7-513; in Battle of Gettysburg, 7-522

Lopez, Narciso: invades Cuba, 6-413, 432

Louis XVI, King of France: aids Americans in Revolution, 2-145

Louisbourg: in King George's War, 2-92

Louisiana: named for Louis XIV, 1-68; ceded to Spain, 2-101; regained by French, 3-232; territory purchased by Jefferson,

L (contd.)

3-235

Lovejoy, Reverend Elijah P.: abolitionist editor, 5-360

Lowell, James Russell: American writer, 7-544

Lowndes, William: 4-271

Loyalists: in Revolutionary War, 2-134, 154

Ludendorff, General Erich von: favors resumption of unrestricted submarine warfare, 11-829; in March, 1918 offensive, 11-846; threatens Paris, 11-847, 848; in Second Battle of the Marne, 11-850; concedes defeat, 11-854

Lundy's Lane, Battle of: 4-287

Luniks: Soviet moon rockets, 16-1224

Lusitania: luxury liner makes first voyage, 10-761; sinking of, 11-812-813

Luxembourg: attacked by Germany, 14-1050

M

Mac Arthur, General Douglas: becomes Philippine Commonwealth military advisor, 13-986; and fall of Philippines, 14-1071; returns to Philippines, 14-1103, 1106; and Japanese surrender, 14-1115; named commander of U.N. forces in Korea, 15-1162; and invasion of Inchon, 15-1163; confers with President Truman, 15-1165; recalled by President Truman, 15-1166; in "Great Debate," 15-1167

MacDonald, J. Ramsay: and London Naval Conference, 12-937

Macdonough, Captain Thomas: 4-287

Macmillan, Harold: 16-1225, 1228

Macon's Bill Number 2: 4-267

Madero, Francisco: 10-790

Madison, Dolly: becomes First Lady, 4-264; and burning of Washington, 4-288

Madison, James: reports Constitutional Convention, 3-177; comments on Constitution, 3-183; drafts Virginia Resolution against Alien and Sedition Acts, 3-219; appointed Secretary of State, 3-229; elected fourth President, 4-264; reopens trade with France, 4-267; annexes West Florida, 4-268; asks for armed forces, 4-271; and declaration of War of 1812, 4-273; reelected, 4-274; appoints new Secretary of War, 4-278; accepts mediation offer, 4-284; flees Washington, 4-288; signs Bank bill, 4-294; recommends federal highways, 4-296; vetoes road building bill, 4-296

Magellan, Ferdinand: circles world, 1-22

Mahan, Captain Alfred T.: naval historian, 9-661

Maine: U. S. battleship sinks at Havana, 9-698

Makin Island: 14-1095

Malenkov, Georgi M.: replaces Stalin, 15-1178

Manchuria: taken by Japan, 12-943

Manhattan Island: first reached by Verrazano, 1-25; Dutch occupation, 1-50

Manifest Destiny: 6-417

Manila, Philippine Islands: 9-704; falls to Japanese, 14-1071; recaptured, 14-1106

Manila Bay, Battle of: 9-700

Mann, A. Dudley: 6-414

Mann, Horace: improves standards of public schooling, 5-362

Mann-Elkins Act: 10-781

Mao Tse-tung: 15-1159

Marbury, William: 3-231

Marcy, William: 6-430

Mariana Islands: 12-894; 14-1102

Marin, Louis Munoz: 15-1179

Marine Corps: established, 3-217; women's unit of Marines organized, 14-1085

Mariner IV: takes photos of Mars, 16-1258

Marion, General Francis: "Swamp Fox" leads Rangers, 2-147

Marne, Second Battle of: 11-850

Marquette, Father Jacques: explores Mississippi River, 1-62

Marshall, George C.: army chief of staff, 14-1072; initiates European Recovery Plan, 15-1138; and Latin American aid, 15-1150; attempts to mediate in China, 15-1159

Marshall, John: acts as peace envoy to France, 3-214; appointed Chief Justice, 3-231; and Yazoo land sales, 4-268; invokes implied powers, 4-302, 304; rules on Indian question, 5-339

Marshall Islands: 12-894; 14-1102

Marshall Plan: 15-1138

Maryland: founded by Lord Baltimore, 1-53; remains loyal to Union, 7-496

Mason, James M.: and Trent affair, 7-500

Mason, James Y.: 6-430

Massachusetts Bay Colony: 1-51

Massachusetts Colony: 1-47

Massasoit: 1-48, 49

Mather, Cotton: early American writer, 1-72

Matsu: 15-1159; 16-1217

Maximilian: Archduke of Austria becomes Mexican Emperor, 7-531; executed, 8-584

Mayflower: 1-47; Mayflower Compact, 1-47

Maysville-Lexington Turnpike Road: in federal aid controversy, 5-333

McAdoo, William G.: assumes control of railroads, 11-843

McAfee, Captain Mildred H.: heads WAVES, 14-1084

McCarran Internal Security Act: 15-1164

McCarthy, Joseph R.: heads committee investigating Communist activities, 15-1160

McClellan, General George B.: attacks Confederates at Philippi, 7-496; appointed commander-in-chief of Union Army, 7-498; in Peninsular Campaign, 7-510; recalled to Washington, 7-511; attempts to block Lee's invasion of the North, 7-515; loses command of troops, 7-516; in election of 1864, 7-534, 540

McCloy, John J.: American diplomat, 15-1157

McCormick, Cyrus Hall: invents reaper, 5-345

McCormick Harvester Works: and labor troubles, 9-660

McCulloch versus Maryland: shows Supreme Court position on United States' supremacy, 4-302

McDivitt, James: command pilot of Gemini 4, 16-1259

McDowell, General Irvin: at First Battle of Bull Run, 7-497; in Peninsula Campaign, 7-510

McKinley, William: nominated for President, 9-693; elected, 9-695; and tariff, 9-676, 696; and Cuban crisis, 9-698; asks for war against Spain, 9-699; and Hawaiian annexation, 9-703; reelected, 9-714; assassinated, 10-734

McKinley Tariff: raises duties to all-time high, 9-676; effect on Hawaiian economy, 9-683

McLoughlin, John: 4-263

McNary-Haugen Bill: 12-930

McNutt, Paul V.: 14-1072

McParlan, James: 8-617

Meade, General George C.: replaces Hooker as commander, 7-521

Meany, George: 15-1189

Mechanicsville, Battle of: 7-511

Mellon, Andrew: opposes League of Nations, 11-862

Memorial Day: 8-588

Mencken, H. L.: writer, 12-935

Menendez de Aviles, Pedro: 1-33

Mercantilism: 1-60

Meredith, James M.: in University of Mississippi integration, 16-1243

Merrimac: taken by Confederates, 7-494; renamed Virginia, and engages Monitor, 7-505

Mesabi Range: 5-374

Meuse-Argonne offensive: 11-852

Mexico: and early Spanish explorers, 1-23, 26, 30; and Texas revolution, 5-351-353; and annexation of Texas, 5-380; breaks relations with United States, 5-381; at war with United States, 5-382, 386, 389; defeated and signs Treaty of Guadalupe-Hidalgo, 5-389; occupied by French troops, 7-531; and crisis over Maximilian, 8-574; and death of Maximilian, 8-584; and relations with United States, 10-790-791; and Zimmermann note, 11-832; and Good Neighbor Policy, 12-922, 928

Mexico City: captured by Cortez, 1-23; and Coronado, 1-30; captured by Scott, 5-389

Michelson, Abraham: wins Nobel Prize for Physics, 12-900

Middle East Treaty Organization (METO): 15-1188

Midway, Battle of: 14-1079

Milan Decree of 1807: 4-260

Miller, Thomas W.: in Harding scandals, 12-906

Millikan, Robert A.: wins Nobel Prize for Physics, 12-900

Mill Springs, Battle of: 7-503

Miller, William E.: defeated for Vice-President in 1964, 16-1256

Mint, United States: established, 3-197

Minuit, Peter: 1-50

Minutemen: 2-121, 123

Missionaries, Spanish: 1-31

Missions, Spanish: 1-31

Mississippi, University of: and integration crisis, 16-1243

Missouri: admitted to Union, 4-305; and Kansas question, 6-427, 431; and Dred Scott Case, 6-440, 476

Missouri Compromise: 4-303; and the Dred Scott Decision, 6-440, 476

Mitchell, John: in Pennsylvania coal strike, 10-740

Mitchell, General William (Billy) L.: defends air power, 12-913

Mobile Bay, Battle of: 7-538

Molly Maguires: secret order of labor terrorists, 8-617

Molotov, Vyacheslav M.: 14-1092, 1109; 15-1143

Monitor: engages warship Virginia (Merrimac), 7-505

Monroe, James: United States minister to France, 3-210; negotiates Louisiana Purchase, 3-235; elected fifth President, 4-295; reelected, 4-304; favors recognition of new Latin-American republics, 4-306; proclaims Monroe Doctrine, 4-307

Monroe Doctrine: 4-307; 6-429; 10-745, 752

Montcalm, Marquis de: at Quebec, 2-97

Montezuma: 1-23

Montgomery, General Bernard L.: 14-1080

Montgomery, Alabama: and Confederate Convention, 7-490; and bus boycott, 15-1191

Montreal, Canada: 1-40, 62; 2-97

Mooney, Thomas J.: and Preparedness Day bombing, 11-823

Moore, John Bassett: 12-952

Moore's Creek Bridge, Battle of: 2-134

Morgan, General Daniel: 2-150

Morgan, J. Pierpont: aids government in gold crisis, 9-692; testifies on money trusts, 10-784; and German reparations, 12-929

Morgan, William: and Anti-Masonic Party, 5-337

Mormons: 5-387; 6-451

Morocco: 3-181; 10-756

Morrill Land Grant Act: 7-512

Morris, Gouverneur: 3-177

Morris, Robert: helps finance the

M (contd.)

Revolution, 2·140; recommends Hamilton for Treasury post, 3·187

Morristown: Washington's winter camp, 2·138

Morrow, Dwight W.: 12·922

Morse, Samuel F. B.: 5·376

Mosby, Colonel John S.: Confederate raider, 7·536

Moscow Conference of Foreign Ministers: 14·1092

Mosquito War: 6·429

Motion pictures: and development of sound, 12·920

Mott, Lucretia: and women's rights, 5·395; in abolition movement, 6·411; in suffrage movement, 6·460

Mount Holyoke Seminary: founded, 5·395

"Muckrakers": reform writers, 10·757; attack Taft's tariff policy, 10·771; in conservation dispute, 10·772

Muhlenberg, F. A. C.: 3·184

Mulligan Letters: in election of 1884, 9·657

Munich Pact: and appeasement of Hitler, 13·1024

Murray, Philip: labor leader, 13·1025

Mussolini, Benito: attacks Ethiopia, 13·1001; joins Hitler in Rome-Berlin Axis, 13·1005; at Munich, 13·1024; attacks Albania, 13·1028; attacks France, 14·1052; overthrown, 14·1090; heads rump Italian government, 14·1091; death of, 14·1110

N

Nagasaki: 14·1114

Nagy, Imre: 15·1192

Napoleon Bonaparte: comes into power, 3·217; regains Louisiana for France, 3·234; sells Louisiana Territory to United States, 3·235; blockades British Isles, 4·255; agreement with Czar, 4·260; sends Cadore to America, 4·267; overthrown, 4·286

Napoleon III: places Maximilian on Mexican throne, 7·531; withdraws troops from Mexico, 8·574

Narvaez, Panfilo: 1·26

Nashville, Battle of: 7·545

Nasser, Gamal Abdel: 15·1190; 16·1215

Nation, Carrie: crusades for temperance, 10·731

National Defense Education Act: 16·1218

National Farmers' Alliance of the Northwest: organizes Populist Party, 9·678

National Industrial Recovery Act: provides for organization of industry under codes, 13·978; declared unconstitutional, 13·996

National Labor Relations Act: 13·998

National Labor Union: organized, 8·576

National Recovery Administration: 13·978; discontinued, 13·996

National Republican Party: 4·309; 5·340

National Security Act: unifies armed forces, 15·1141

National Security Council: created, 15·1141

National Security Resources Board: 15·1141

National Socialist (Nazi) Party: 13·972

National Trades Union: formation, 5·346

National War Labor Board: 14·1072, 1088

National Youth Administration: 13·997

Naturalization Act: 3·218

Nautilus: makes first underseas polar crossing, 16·1216

Navajo Indians: 1·64

Navigation Acts: 2·110

Navy, United States: created, 2·129; Department established, 3·217; women's unit, WAVES, organized, 14·1084

Nebraska: and popular sovereignty, 6·426; and Kansas-Nebraska Act, 6·427

Negroes: arrive in America, 1·45; in the Constitution, 3·178; and the invention of the cotton gin, 3·203; in Census of 1800, 3·227; and Santo Domingo revolt, 3·234; end of importation of slaves, 4·262; and Compromise of 1820, 4·303; Nat Turner's rebellion, 5·336; and beginnings of abolition movement, 5·349; anti-slavery petitions, 5·357; Amistad revolt, 5·364; in Census of 1840, 5·366; Creole mutiny, 5·369; Dickens criticizes slavery, 5·370; Wilmot Proviso, 5·384; in Census of 1850, 5·394; and Compromise of 1850, 5·396; situation in 1850, 6·409, 410; Fugitive Slave Act, 6·410; and abolition movement, 6·411; Dred Scott decision, 6·440; and slavery system, 6·442, 443; Crittenden proposal, 6·473; situation in 1860, 6·476; and constitution of the Confederacy, 7·490; emancipation movement, 7·501, 514, 517, 518; Freedmen's Bureau, 7·548; Thirteenth Amendment, 7·556; Black Codes, 8·572; Civil Rights Act 1866, 8·573; Fourteenth Amendment, 8·575; enrolled as voters, 8·582; in Southern legislatures, 8·589; Fifteenth Amendment, 8·598; and Klu Klux Klan beginnings, 8·599; in Census of 1870, 8·600; Civil Rights Law 1875, 8·613; in Census of 1880, 8·635; with Peary at North Pole, 10·770; and Klu Klux Klan, 12·901; and culture of 1920's, 12·935; in Census of 1930, 12·940; school segregation declared unconstitutional, 15·1184; bus boycotts, 15·1191; Civil Rights Act 1957, 16·1210; Little Rock

incident, 16·1211; Meredith enters U. of Mississippi, 16·1243; march on Washington, D.C., 16·1249; Civil Rights Act, 1964, 16·1257

Nelson, Donald M.: 14·1072

Netherland: in New World, 1·50; attacked by Germany 14·1050

Neutrality: 3·201, 207, 211; 5·361; 10·793; 13·1000, 1001, 1011, 1023

Nevada: and Comstock Lode, 6·453

New Amsterdam: 1·50

New England Confederation: 1·58

Newfoundland: sighted by Cabot, 1·18; touched by Verrazano, 1·25; explored by Cartier, 1·28

New France: 1·40

New Frontier: Kennedy program, 16·1234

New Guinea: invaded, 14·1094

Newlands Reclamation Act: 10·741

"New Lights": colonial religious group, 2·91

New Mexico: ceded to United States, 5·389; admitted as state, 10·777

New Netherland: expansion of, 1·50; seized by England, 1·61

New Orleans, Louisiana: occupied by Union forces, 7·508

New Orleans, Battle of: 4·292

Nicaragua: and "dollar diplomacy," 10·776, 11·818; and United States intervention, 12·922

Nicholas II, Czar of Russia: calls Hague peace conference, 9·707

Nicolls, Colonel Richard: 1·61

Nimitz, Admiral Chester W.: 14·1079, 1102

Nina: Columbus' vessel, 1·14

Nixon, Richard M.: in 1952 campaign, 15·1176; in 1956 campaign, 15·1194; and South American tour, 16·1214; in Kennedy debates, 16·1229; defeated for President, 16·1230

Nomura, Kichisaburo: 14·1068, 1069

Non-Importation Act: 4·255

Non-Intercourse Act: 4·262, 265

Normandy: invasion of, 14·1096

Norris-La Guardia Anti-Injunction Act: 12·949

North Atlantic Treaty Organization (NATO): 15·1155

Northern Securities Company Case: Supreme Court ruling against railroad trust, 10·750

Northwest Ordinance of 1787: 3·179

Northwest Passage: 1·50

Northwest Territory: and Ordinance of 1785, 3·172; and Ordinance of 1787, 3·179; and Indian problems, 3·198

Norway: attacked by Germany, 14·1050

Nullification: 4·314; 5·331, 332, 341, 342

Nuremberg, Germany: war crimes trials, 14·1116, 15·1143

Nye, Gerald P.: conducts hearings on war causes, 13·1000

O

Oberlin College: 5·349

Office of Censorship: 14·1075

Office of Civilian Defense: 14·1075

Office of Economic Stabilization: established, 15·1131

Office of Price Administration (OPA): 14·1075

Office of War Information: 14·1075

Office of War Mobilization: 14·1088

Oglethorpe, James: founds Georgia, 1·74

Oil: and drilling of first well, 6·456

Okinawa, Battle of: 14·1107

Oklahoma District: and sale of homesteads, 9·668-669

Oklahoma "Sooners": 9·669

Old Ironsides: in War of 1812, 4·279

"Old Lights": colonial religious group, 2·91

Olney, Richard: acts in Pullman strike, 9·690; role in Venezuelan boundary dispute, 9·709

Omnibus Act: restores seven Southern states to Union, 8·589

Omnibus Bill: provides for admission of four states, 9·668

O'Neill, Eugene: American playwright, 13·1026

Open Door Notes: 9·708, 712

Order of the Star Spangled Banner: 6·417

Ordinance of 1785: 3·172

Ordinance of 1787: 3·179

Oregon: issue in election of 1844, 5·379; boundaries established, 5·383; and boundary settlement, 8·602

Oregon Trail: route of Márcus Whitman, 5·355; in California gold rush, 5·392

Organization of American States (OAS): provides collective security, 15·1150

Orlando, Vittorio: at Paris peace conference, 11·856

Ostend Manifesto: on Cuba, 6·430; and Republican Party, 6·437

Otis, Harrison G.: and Hartford Convention, 4·291

Otis, James: fights Writs of Assistance, 2·98

Ottawa Indians: 2·103

Overland Mail Company: 6·463

Owen, Robert Dale: 5·330

P

Pacific Telegraph Act: 6·463

Pact of Paris: see Kellogg-Briand Pact

Paine, Thomas: writes Common Sense, 2·130

Pakenham, General Edward: 4·292

Palmer, A. Mitchell: acts in coal strike of 1919, 11·865; conducts campaign against radicals, 11·866

Panama, Republic of: established after revolt against Colombia, 10·748

Panama Canal: background of United States' involvement, 10·736; Spooner Act appropriates funds, 10·742; construction of, 10·760; opened, 10·794

Panama Conference (1939): and hemispheric solidarity, 13·1035

P (contd.)

Panama Congress (1826): called by Bolivar, **4**·311
Pan-American Conference (1881): **9**·652, 673
Pan-American Union: **9**·673
Panay Incident: sinking of American gunboat in China, **13**·1017
Panics: of 1819, **4**·300; of 1837, **5**·359; of 1857, **6**·441; of 1873, **8**·611; of 1893, **9**·685
Papen, Captain Franz von: in World War I sabotage, **11**·817
Parcel post: becomes part of postal service, **10**·781
Paris: liberation of in World War II, **14**·1099
Paris, Treaty of (1898): ends Spanish-American War, **9**·705
Parker, Alton B.: nominated by Democrats to run against Theodore Roosevelt, **10**·751
Patent law: **3**·192
Patrons of Husbandry (Grangers): organized to help farmers, **8**·585
Patroons: **1**·50
Paterson, William: **3**·177
Patton, General George S. Jr.: **14**·1086, 1090, 1096
Pauling, Linus C.: **15**·1175
Payne-Aldrich Tariff: **10**·771, 788
Peace Corps: established, **16**·1239
"Peace Ship": pacifist mission to Europe, **11**·816
Pearl Harbor, Hawaii: attack on, **14**·1069
Peary, Robert E.: reaches North Pole, **10**·770
Peleliu Island: **14**·1102
Pelley, William Dudley: leads "Silver Shirts," **13**·1007
Pendleton, George H.: introduces civil service reform legislation, **9**·654
Peninsular Campaign: of Civil War, **7**·510-511
Penn, William: founds Pennsylvania, **1**·67
Pennsylvania Frame of Government: **1**·67
People's Democratic Republic of Korea: established as northern government, **15**·1161
Pequot Indians' War: **1**·57
Perkins, Frances: becomes Secretary of Labor, **13**·968
Permanent Court of International Arbitration: **9**·707
Permanent Court of International Justice: **12**·952
Perry, Commodore Matthew C.: opens Japan to American trade, **6**·425, 445, 462
Perry, Captain Oliver Hazard: and victory at Lake Erie, **4**·281
Pershing, John J.: pursues Villa in Mexico, **11**·820; appointed commander of American Expeditionary Force, **11**·840; helps stop German drive on Amiens, **11**·846; at Battle of St. Mihiel, **11**·851; in Meuse-Argonne offensive, **11**·852

Peru: conquered by Pizarro, **1**·27; Spanish influence in, **1**·31
Peshtigo, Wisconsin: fire of 1871, **8**·604
Petain, Marshal Henri-Philippe. **14**·1052. 1082
Petersburg, Battle of: **7**·550
Philadelphia, Pennsylvania: site of Constitutional Convention, **3**·177; early capital of United States, **3**·195; suffers yellow fever plague, **3**·202; holds Centennial, **8**·620-621
Philip II, King of Spain: **1**·38
Philippi, Battle of: **7**·496
Philippine Islands: and Magellan, **1**·22; and Spanish-American War, **9**·700, 702, 704, 705, 706; and Organic Act creating government, **10**·743; granted increased autonomy, **11**·824; creation of commonwealth, **13**·986; conquered by Japanese, **14**·1071; and return of MacArthur, **14**·1106; proclaimed independent, **15**·1134; and United States aid, **15**·1135
Philippine Sea, Battle of: **14**·1102
Phillips, Wendell: **6**·411
Photographs: trans-Atlantic transmission of, **12**·909
Pickering, John: **4**·252
Pickett's Charge: **7**·522
Pierce, Franklin: in 1852 election, **6**·418; fourteenth President, **6**·422; signs Kansas-Nebraska bill, **6**·427; and Kansas, **6**·431, 434, 436
Pike, Zebulon M.: discovers Pike's Peak, **4**·259; killed, **4**·283
Pilgrims: leave England, **1**·47; sign Mayflower Compact, **1**·47; land at Plymouth, **1**·48; hold thanksgiving service, **1**·49
Pinchot, Gifford: named chairman of conservation commission, **10**·765; in conservation dispute, **10**·773
Pinckney, Charles C.: envoy to France, **3**·214; Presidential nominee, **3**·225; in 1804 election, **4**·254; in 1808 election, **4**·264
Pinckney, Thomas: negotiates Treaty of San Lorenzo, **3**·210; candidate for Vice-President, **3**·213
Pinkney, William: **4**·255
Pinta: Spanish vessel, **1**·14
Pioneer IV: American rocket orbits sun, **16**·1224
Pioneer V: radio satellite, **16**·1226
Pitt, William: strengthens army in America, **2**·97; shows sympathy towards Americans, **2**·109
Pizarro, Francisco: in Peru, **1**·27
Plains Indians: **1**·64
Plains of Abraham: **2**·97
Platt Amendment: limits Cuban independence, **10**·733, 738
Plymouth, Massachusetts: second English colony, **1**·47; reached by Pilgrims, **1**·48; celebrates Thanksgiving, **1**·49
Pocahontas: and John Smith, **1**·41
Point Four Program: **15**·1154
Poland: threatened by Hitler, **13**·1028; attacked by Germany,

13·1031; and anti-Communist riots, **15**·1192
Political parties: beginning of two-party system, **3**·204; emergence of Democrats, **4**·315, **5**·328; formation of Republican Party, **6**·428
Polk, James K.: elected President, **5**·379; and Oregon Treaty, **5**·383; refuses renomination, **5**·390
Polo, Marco: **1**·8
Pontiac: and Indian rebellion, **2**·103
Pony Express: **6**·463
Poor Richard's Almanack: **2**·95
Pope, General John: in Mississippi River campaign, **7**·506, 507; at Second Battle of Bull Run, **7**·513
Popular sovereignty: in Utah and New Mexico, **6**·408; and Compromise of 1850, **6**·426; and Kansas-Nebraska Act, **6**·427; as issue in 1860, **6**·468
Populist Party: agrarian political organization, **9**·678; nominates Bryan, **9**·693
Port Arthur, Manchuria: and defeat of Russians by Japan, **10**·755
Porter, Peter B.: **4**·271
Portsmouth, New Hampshire: treaty signed ending Russo-Japanese War, **10**·755
Portugal: world maritime leader, **1**·10; seeks route to Orient, **1**·11; and Line of Demarcation, **1**·16
Postal savings banks: **10**·781
Post Office: established, **4**·266
Potsdam Conference: **14**·1113
Powers, Francis Gary: flies U-2 plane over Soviet Union, **16**·1227; convicted of espionage, **16**·1228
Powhatan, **1**·41
"Prayer of Twenty Millions": emancipation plea written by Horace Greeley, **7**·514
Preble, Edward: **3**·230
Presidential Succession Act: of 1886, **9**·659; of 1947, **15**·1140
Pribilof Islands: and sealing question, **9**·686
Price, Byron: **14**·1075
Proclamation Line of 1763: **2**·102
Prohibition: amendment ratified, **11**·857; and crime, **12**·941; repealed, **13**·983
Providence, Rhode Island: established by Roger Williams, **1**·55
Public Credit Act: **8**·601
Public Works Administration: **13**·978
Pueblo Indians: **1**·64
Puerto Rico: ceded to United States, **9**·705; government of, **10**·732; becomes territory of United States, **11**·833; becomes commonwealth, **15**·1179
Pujo, Arsene P.: **10**·784
Pulaski, Count Casimir: helps Washington in Revolutionary War: **2**·140
Pulitzer, Joseph: and role of press in Cuban revolt, **9**·697
Pullman, George M.: and railroad strike, **9**·690
Puritans: at Salem, **1**·51, 52
Pusan, Battle of: **15**·1163

Pu-Yi, Henry: **12**·945

Q

Quakers: in Pennsylvania, **1**·67
Quebec: founded by Champlain, **1**·40; and defeat of French, **2**·97
Quebec Conference: **14**·1092
Queenston Heights, Battle of: **4**·277
Quemoy: **15**·1159; **16**·1217
Quezon, Manuel: becomes first president of Philippine Commonwealth, **13**·986
Quids: **3**·209, 232
Quinn, William F.: **16**·1222

R

Radical Republicans: **7**·501, **7**·517, **7**·534, **7**·535
Radio: as wartime aid, **11**·810; development of broadcasting, **11**·874; growth of, **13**·991
Railroad Labor Board: **11**·868
Railroads: transcontinental line completed, **8**·594; operation during World War I, **11**·843; returned to private owners, **11**·868
Railroad strikes: of 1877, **8**·627; of 1946, **15**·1133
Raleigh, Sir Walter: **1**·36, 37
Randolph, Edmund: at Constitutional Convention, **3**·177; named Attorney General, **3**·186
Randolph, John: opposes Georgia cession of land, **3**·209; opposes Jefferson's policies, **3**·232; and Bank of the United States, **4**·269; and Panama issue, **4**·311
Rangers: in Revolutionary War, **2**·147
Rankin, Jeannette: becomes first woman to be elected to Congress, **11**·834
Reaper: invention of, **5**·345
Recession: temporary economic setback of 1937, **13**·1018
Reconstruction: Lincoln's plan, **7**·535, 549; **8**·570; Johnson's program, **7**·554; Radical Republican attitude, **8**·571, 575; ends, **8**·626
Reconstruction Finance Corporation: **12**·946, **13**·973
Recreation: in colonies, **2**·104; on frontier, **2**·105; in "Roaring Twenties," **12**·936
Reed, Dr. Walter: fights yellow fever, **9**·713
Reed, William B.: **6**·446
Reeder, Andrew H.: in Kansas controversy, **6**·427, 431, 434
"Regulators" of North Carolina: **2**·114
Reorganization Act: effects changes in executive department, **15**·1156
Reparations: becomes problem after World War I, **12**·903, 929, 944
Republic of Korea: **15**·1161
Resettlement Administration: plans suburban communities, **13**·1014
Reuther, Walter: **15**·1189
Revere, Paul: alerts colonists, **2**·122; as post rider, **4**·266
Revivalist movements: **2**·91, **3**·223
Revolutionary War: background,

R (contd.)
causes and early actions, 2-108-131; Declaration of Independence, 2-132; battles, 2-135-153; peace treaty, 2-154

Reynaud, Paul: 14-1052

Rezanov, Nicholas P.: 3-221

Rhee, Syngman: 15-1161, 1181

Rhode Island: founded, 1-55; trading problems in, 3-176; suffrage controversy, 5-372

Rhodes, Cecil: 10-739

Richardson, William A.: 8-609

Richmond, Virginia: attack on, 7-532-533

Rickenbacker, Edward: 11-849

Rickover, Rear Admiral Hyman G.: 16-1216

Ridgway, General Matthew B.: 15-1166

Rio de Janeiro Conference: 14-1074

Rio de Janeiro Treaty: strengthens hemispheric relations, 15-1142

Roanoke Island Colony: first British colony, 1-36, 37

"Roaring Twenties": begin 11-872-873; results of exciting decade, 12-940

Robin Moor: sunk, 14-1063

Robinson, James: 3-170

Robinson, Joseph T.: 12-926

Rochambeau, Comte de: 2-151

Rockefeller, John D.: and Standard Oil empire, 8-631; organizes trust, 9-653; trust ordered dissolved, 9-679

Rodgers, Captain John: 4-270

Roebling, John A.: 9-655

Rogers, Will: 12-936

Rokossovsky, General Konstantin: 14-1087

Rolfe, John: 1-41, 1-44, 45

Rommel, General Erwin: 14-1080

Roosevelt, Eleanor: 13-969; 15-1130

Roosevelt, Franklin D.: in election of 1920, 11-869; and Presidential campaign of 1932, 12-953-954; elected President, 12-955; launches New Deal, 13-968-969; declares bank holiday, 13-970; delivers first fireside chat, 13-970; and London Economic Conference, 13-977; promotes Good Neighbor Policy, 13-984; abandons gold standard, 13-985; fosters collective security, 13-1000; reelected in 1936, 13-1009; and Supreme Court plan, 13-1010; and Sino-Japanese conflict, 13-1013; asks quarantine of aggressors, 13-1016; and two-ocean navy, 13-1021; and Fair Labor Standards Act, 13-1023; heeds Einstein on atomic weapons, 13-1029; asks Western Hemisphere solidarity, 13-1034; aids democracies, 14-1048; strengthens American defense, 14-1053; and destroyer-bases deal, 14-1056; supports draft, 14-1057; and 1940 election, 14-1057, 1060; delivers Four Freedoms speech, 14-1061;

applies oil embargo on Japan, 14-1065; and Atlantic Charter, 14-1066; issues "shoot on sight" order, 14-1067; asks revision of Neutrality Act, 14-1067; and Japanese "peace" mission, 14-1068; asks declaration of war, 14-1070; and policy of unconditional surrender, 14-1083; at Quebec Conference, 14-1092; at Teheran and Cairo Conferences, 14-1093; elected for fourth term, 14-1100; at Yalta Conference, 14-1104; death of, 14-1108

Roosevelt, Theodore: asks action against Spanish, 9-698; directs navy against Spain, 9-700; and Rough Riders at San Juan Hill, 9-701; elected Vice-President, 9-714; inaugurated as President, 10-735; acts in coal strike, 10-740; encourages conservation, 10-741; in Venezuelan debt controversy, 10-744, 745; acts against trusts, 10-746, 750; "big stick" diplomacy, 10-747; elected in 1904, 10-751; announces Corollary to Monroe Doctrine, 10-752; mediates Russo-Japanese War and receives Nobel Peace Prize, 10-755; and Algeciras conference, 10-756; and "muckrakers," 10-757; asks for international court, 10-762; concludes "Gentlemen's Agreement" with Japan, 10-764; calls conservation conference, 10-765; orders fleet around the world, 10-768; encourages Boy Scout movement, 10-774; questions Taft's policies, 10-775; nominated by Progressives, 10-779; loses in election of 1912, 10-780; and World War I, 11-840

Roosevelt, Lieutenant Colonel Theodore, Jr.: organizes American Legion, 11-859

Roosevelt Corollary: 10-752, 754

Root, Elihu: 10-733, 735, 12-952

Root-Takahira Agreement: outlines policy in Far East, 10-767

Rosecrans, General William S.: at Chickamauga, 7-524

Rosenbergs, Julius and Ethel: executed for espionage, 15-1164

Ross, General Robert: 4-288

Roxas, Manuel: 15-1134

Rumsey, James: 3-182

Rundstedt, General Karl von: 14-1101

Rural Electrification Administration: 13-995

Rush, Doctor Benjamin: 3-202

Rush, Richard: and Rush-Bagot agreement, 4-297; in 1828 election, 4-315

Rush-Bagot agreement: 4-297

Russell, Jonathan, 4-284

Russell, Major and Waddell Company: 6-463

Russia: gains foothold in North America, 3-221; and American fur trade, 4-263; offers to mediate War of 1812, 4-284; and Monroe

Doctrine, 4-307; sells Alaska to United States, 8-583; in war with Japan, 10-755; in Second Hague Conference, 10-762; and causes of World War I, 11-808-809; and overthrow of Czar, 11-835; and effects of revolution in United States, 11-866; Allied intervention in, 11-867; and famine of 1921, 12-893; recognized by United States, 13-980; aids Spanish Loyalists, 13-1011; signs pact with Germany, 13-1030; seizes Polish territory, 13-1031; invades Finland, 13-1033; invaded by Germany, 14-1064; in Battle of Stalingrad, 14-1087; at Dumbarton Oaks Conference, 14-1098; expels Germans, 14-1099; drives to Berlin, 14-1110; declares war on Japan, 14-1114; signs treaty with China, 14-1115; at Council of Foreign Ministers meeting, 14-1116; in early U.N. controversies, 15-1130; and atomic energy control, 15-1132; and satellite treaties, 15-1136; attitude toward Marshall Plan, 15-1138; disagreement on German question, 15-1143; absorbs satellites, 15-1144; and Berlin blockade, 15-1147; intensifies Cold War, 15-1149; and Lend-Lease, 15-1149; and German Democratic Republic, 15-1157; explodes atomic bomb, 15-1158; asks cease-fire and armistice in Korea, 15-1172; and Suez crisis, 15-1190; signs "Atoms for Peace" agreement, 15-1193; puts first satellite into orbit, 16-1212; launches moon rocket, 16-1224; and Summit conference, 16-1228; places first man in orbit around earth, 16-1235; accomplishes seventeen orbits of earth, 16-1239; and Berlin Wall, 16-1240

Russian-American Company: gets Alaskan Charter, 3-221

Russo-Japanese War: 10-755

Ruth, Babe: 11-873, 12-936

Ryukus Islands: 14-1107

S

Sabotage: during World War I, 11-817

Sacco, Nicola: 12-919

St. Augustine, Florida: 1-33

St. Clair, General Arthur: 3-198

St. Lawrence River: and voyages of Cartier, 1-28; settlements by Champlain, 1-40

St. Lawrence Seaway: 16-1221

St. Leger, Colonel Barry: 2-141

St. Mihiel, Battle of: 11-851

Saipan, Battle of: 14-1102

"Salary Grab" Act: 8-609

Salem, Massachusetts: established by Puritans, 1-51; and witch trials, 1-69

Salk, Jonas E.: 15-1186

Salomon, Haym: 2-140

Samoa: three-power protectorate established, 9-671; partitioned,

9-707

Sampson, Admiral William T.: commands Atlantic fleet, 9-700; at Santiago, 9-702

Sanders, George N.: 6-417

Sanford, John D.: in Grant scandals, 8-609

Sanford, John F. A.: 6-440

San Francisco, California: in earthquake of 1906, 10-758; in Preparedness Day bombing, 11-823

San Francisco Conference: 14-1109

Sanger, Thomas: 8-617

San Jacinto: British ship in Trent affair, 7-500

San Juan Hill, Battle of: 9-701

San Lorenzo, Treaty of: 3-210

San Salvador: 1-15

Santa Anna, General: lays siege to Alamo, 5-351; captures Alamo, 5-352; capture of, 5-353; in Mexican War, 5-389

Santo Domingo: See Dominican Rep.

Saratoga, Battle of: surrender of Burgoyne, 2-142; and French alliance, 2-145

Satellite peace treaties: 15-1136

"Scalawags": Southern collaborators in Congressional reconstruction plan, 8-569

Schechter Case: and National Industrial Recovery Act, 13-996

Schirra, Commander Walter M. Jr.: orbits earth six times, 16-1251

Schley, Commodore Winfield S.: 9-702

Schofield, General John M.: 7-545

Schurz, Carl: 6-414

Schuschnigg, Kurt: 13-1020

Scopes, John T.: 12-911

Scott, General Charles: 3-198

Scott, Dred: sues for freedom, 6-440; and Supreme Court decision, 6-476

Scott, Howard: 13-1006

Scott, General Winfield: leads attack on Canada, 4-283, 286; commands forces in South Carolina, 5-342; in Caroline affair, 5-361; in Aroostook War, 5-363; in Mexican War, 5-389; in election of 1852; 6-418; and Compromise of 1850, 6-422

Seabees: 14-1089

Sea Dogs: 1-34, 38.

Sealing: and Bering Sea controversy, 9-686

Secession: claimed constitutional by South, 6-459; South Carolina leads South into, 6-474

Second Continental Congress: meets in Philadelphia, 2-125; and Declaration of Independence, 2-132; and Articles of Confederation, 2-153

Second Hague International Conference: 10-762

Securities and Exchange Commission: 13-988

Security Council: members, 15-1130; acts on Korea, 15-1162

Sedition Act (1798): passed by Congress, 3-218; becomes issue

S (contd.)

in states' rights, 3·219; in campaign of 1800, 3·226; (1918) tightens American security in World War I, 11·845
Selective Service Act: 11·839
Semmes, Captain Raphael: 7·509
Separatists: 1·47
Sergeant, John: 4·311
Servicemen's Readjustment Act (G.I. Bill of Rights): 14·1097
Seven Cities of Cibola: 1·30
Seven Days' Battles: 7·511
Seventeenth Amendment: provides for direct election of senators, 10·787
Seven Years' War: 2·94, 99
Sevier, John: 3·170
Seward, William H.: and Irrepressible Conflict, 6·450; in 1860 election, 6·461, 465; appointed Secretary of State, 7·491; and English recognition of South, 7·495; in Trent affair, 7·500; helps maintain English neutrality, 7·517; denounces French violation of Monroe Doctrine in Mexico, 7·531; warns Austria on Mexican expedition, 8·574; and purchase of Alaska, 8·583
Sewing machine: invention of, 5·385; and influence on industry, 6·420
Shafter, General William: 9·701
Shanghai, China: attacked by Japanese, 12·945
Shannon, Wilson: 6·431, 6·436
Shays, Daniel: 3·175
Shelikhov, Gregory: 3·221
Shepard, Commander Alan B., Jr.: makes first American sub-orbital **flight, 16·1237**
Sheridan, General Philip H.: takes over Army of the Shenandoah, 7·536; drives through Shenandoah Valley, 7·543
Sherman, Roger: 3·177
Sherman, General William T.: at Vicksburg, 7·523; march through Georgia, 7·537; march to the sea, 7·542·543; conquest of the Carolinas, 7·547; captures Gen. Johnston's army, 7·552
Sherman Anti-Trust Act: 9·675, 10·750
Sherman Silver Purchase Act: 9·675
Shiloh, Battle of: 7·506
Sholes, Christopher L.: invents first practical typewriter, 8·593
Shriver, R. Sargent: 16·1234
Sicily: invasion of, 14·1090
Sigma 7: Mercury space capsule **orbits earth six times, 16·1244**
Silliman, Benjamin, Jr.: 6·456
Silver question: and "Crime of 1873," 8·608; and Bland-Allison Act, 8·630; and Sherman Act, 9·675; in Populist platform, 9·678; and Panic of 1893, 9·685; and repeal of Purchase Act, 9·687; and campaigns of 1896, 9·693; and depression of 1930's, 13·992
Sinclair, Harry F.: in Harding

scandals, 12·907
Singer, Isaac M.: 6·420
Sioux Indians: 1·63; go on warpath, 8·614; and Custer's Last Stand, 8·623
Sixteenth Amendment: legalizes federal income tax, 10·783
Skidmore, Thomas: 5·330
Slater, Samuel: introduces cotton goods machinery in America, 3·188, 203
Slaughterhouse cases: Supreme
Slaughterhouse cases: 8·610
Slavery: in colonies, 1·45; and influence of cotton gin, 3·203; and Missouri Compromise, 4·303; and growth of abolitionism, 5·336; in District of Columbia, 5·357; and murder of Lovejoy, 5·360; and slave ship incidents, 5·364, 369; and Wilmot Proviso, 5·384; and Compromise of 1850, 5·396; and question of Cuban annexation, 6·413; and influence of Uncle Tom's Cabin, 6·415; defense of, 6·416, 443; as issue in election of 1852, 6·418-419; in Kansas struggle, 6·426, 427, 428, 431, 434, 436, 437, 438; and Dred Scott decision, 6·440; opposed by Helper, 6·442; in Lincoln-Douglas debates, 6·448-449; and Seward's "Irrepressible Conflict" speech, 6·450; and Vicksburg Convention, 6·454; and Davis resolutions, 6·459; in election of 1860, 6·464-465, 468, 470-471; and secession, 6·472, 474; and Crittenden compromise, 6·473; brings secession, 6·474; and effects of Emancipation Proclamation, 7·518; abolished in United States by Thirteenth Amendment, 7·556
Slidell, John: as peace emissary to Mexico, 5·382; and Trent affair, 7·500
Sloat, Commodore John D.: in Mexican War, 5·386
Smith, Alfred E.: nominated for President, 12·926; defeated, 12·927
Smith, Uncle Billy: 6·456
Smith, Captain Edward J.: 10·778
Smith, Gerit: 6·411
Smith, Jesse: 12·907
Smith, Captain John: becomes leader of Jamestown, 1·41
Smith, Joseph: Mormon leader, 5·387
Smith Act: See Alien Registration Act
Smith-Hughes Act: encourages vocational training, 11·831
Smith-Lever Act: creates educational service for farmers, 10·792
Smuggling: among colonists, 2·111
Smyth, General Alexander: 4·277
Social Security Act: 13·999
Soil Conservation Act: 13·1004
Soldiers Bonus Act: 12·904
Solomon Islands: 14·1081, 1094
Songs of the Civil War: 7·502

Sons of Liberty: 2·109 2·111
Soto, Hernando de: 1·29
Soule, Pierre: 6·430
South Carolina: Exposition, 6·439; secedes, 6·474
Southeast Asia Treaty Organization (SEATO): 15·1185
Spaak, Paul-Henri: 15·1130
Space flights: 16·1235, 1237, 1238, 1239, 1241, 1244, 1247, 1259, 1262
Space satellites: 16·1212, 1213, 1219, 1224, 1226, 1242, 1258
Spain: helps Columbus, 1·13; and Line of Demarcation, 1·16; in explorations, 1·20-24, 26, 27, 29-31, 33; and treasure ships, 1·32, 1·34; sends Armada against England, 1·38; enters Revolutionary War on side of colonists, 2·145; prohibits American trade in West Indies, 3·174; and Treaty of San Lorenzo, 3·210; suspends right of deposit at New Orleans, 3·234; cedes East Florida, 4·301; and Latin-American revolts, 4·306; and Monroe Doctrine, 4·307; and slave ship Amistad, 5·364; and Cuban adventure of Lopez, 6·413; and Ostend Manifesto, 6·430; in war with United States, 9·699-706; in Spanish civil war, 13·1005, 1011; visited by Eisenhower, **16·1225**
Spalding, Henry H.: on Oregon Trail, 5·355
Spanish-American War: 9·699-706
Spanish galleons: 1·32, 34
SPARS: women in Coast Guard, 14·1084
Specie Circular: 5·354
Spirit of St. Louis: 12·916-917
Spoils system: origin, 5·329, 8·632, 9·652
Spotsylvania, Battle of: 7·532
Spruance, Admiral Raymond A.: 14·1079, 1102, 1107
Sputnik I: first satellite launched by Russians, 16·1212
Sputnik II: carries dog passenger, 16·1212
Squanto: aids Pilgrims, 1·48
"Square Deal": program of Theodore Roosevelt, 10·740
Stalin, Josef: becomes dictator of Soviet Union, 13·980; signs pact with Hitler, 13·1030; and relations with Germany, 14·1049; demands second front, 14·1092; at Teheran Conference, 14·1093; at Yalta Conference, 14·1104; at Potsdam Conference, 14·1113; death of, 15·1178; denounced by Khrushchev, 15·1192
Stalingrad, Battle of: 14·1087
"Stalwarts": 9·650, 9·656
Stamp Act: arouses colonists to action, 2·108; repealed, 2·109
Stamp Act Congress: 2·108
Standard Oil Company: 8·631, 9·653, 6·679
Standish, Captain Miles: 1·48
Stanton, Edwin M.: appointed

Secretary of War, 7·501; opposes Johnson's reconstruction policy, 8·580; dismissed, 8·586
Stanton, Elizabeth Cady: in reform movement, 5·395; as abolitionist, 6·411; and women's suffrage, 6·460, 8·593
Stanton, Frederick P.: 6·438
Stark, Colonel John: 2·141
Star Spangled Banner: 4·289
State of the Union Message: 3·189
States rights: and Embargo Act, 4·262; and Hartford Convention, 4·291; and South Carolina Exposition, 4·314; and background of struggle, 4·316; and Jackson, 5·329; and Calhoun, 6·439; and Davis resolutions, 6·459; leads to secession, 6·474
Statue of Liberty: 9·662
Steamboat: John Fitch and invention of, 3·182, Robert Fulton and Clermont, 4·258
Steel: processing of, 6·433
Steel strike: of 1892, 9·681; of 1946, 15·1133; of 1952, 15·1174; steel plants seized, 15·1174
Steinbeck, John: 13·1026
Stephens, Alexander H.: makes plea against secession, 6·472; becomes vice-president of Confederacy, 7·490
Stettinius, Edward R. Jr.: at San Francisco Conference, 14·1109; at London Conference, 15·1130; and Japanese peace treaty, 15·1173
Steuben, Friedrich von: 2·140
Stevens, John L.: 9·683
Stevens, Thaddeus: asks severe punishment of South, 8·571
Stevenson, Adlai E.: nominated for President, 15·1176; defeated in 1952 election, 15·1177; renominated, 15·1194; defeated in **1956 election, 15·1195; death of, 16·1260**
1956 election, 15·1195
Stimson, Henry L.: heads American delegation at London Naval Conference, 12·937; and non-recognition policy, 12·945; appointed Secretary of War, 14·1053
Stock market: activities of, 12·932; and disastrous crash, 12·933; and Securities and Exchange Commission, 13·988
Stoddert, Benjamin: 3·217
Stowe, Harriet Beecher: 6·415
Stratton, Lt. Commander Dorothy: heads SPARS, 14·1084
Streeter, Colonel Ruth C.: heads Women Marines, 14·1085
Stuart, General J. E. B.: at Brandy Station, 7·520; death of, 7·532
Stuyvesant, Peter, Dutch governor of New Netherland, 1·61
Submarines: in Revolutionary War, 2·137; in World War II, 14·1089; atomic, 16·1218
Sudetenland: seized by Hitler,

S (contd.)

13·1024

Suffolk Resolves: 2·119
Sullivan, Louis: architect, 12·935
Summit Conference: meeting of Big Four at Geneva, 15·1187; wrecked **by Khrushchev, 16**·1228
Sumner, Charles: 6·435; in Reconstruction, 8·571
Sumter, Fort: surrenders, 7·492
Sun Yat-sen: Chinese statesman of new republic, 10·786
Supreme Court: established, 3·190; and early decisions by John Marshall, 4·268, 302, 304; and Dred Scott, 6·440, 476; reduced by Radical Republicans, 8·579; and Slaughterhouse cases, 8·610; in Granger cases, 9·664; and interstate commerce, 9·675; rules in Insular cases, 10·732; in Northern Securities Case, 10·750; interprets Fourteenth Amendment, 10·753; in Danbury Hatters Case, 10·763; and reorganization plan of F. D. Roosevelt, 13·1010; declares school segregation illegal, 8·574
Surrender of South: terms of, 7·550
Sussex Pledge: German agreement to restrict submarine activity, 11·821
Sutter, Captain John A.: discovery of gold, 5·391

T

Taft, Robert A.: 15·1139.
Taft, William Howard: governor-general of Philippine Islands, 10·735, 743; elected President, 10·766; and tariff question, 10·771; in conservation dispute, 10·772-773; and "dollar diplomacy," 10·776; renominated, 10·779; loses in election of 1912, 10·780
Taft-Hartley Act: 15·1139
Taft-Katsura Memorandum: 10·755
Talleyrand, Duc de: 3·214
Tallmadge, James: 4·303
Tammany Hall Society: 8·607
Taney, Roger B.: Supreme Court Justice, 5·335, 5·343, 6·440, 7·504
Tarawa Island: World War II battlefield, 14·1095
Tariff: of 1789; 3·187; in Clay's American System, 4·308; of Abominations, 4·314, 5·332, 341; and Compromise of 1833, 5·342; Walker, 6·439; of 1857, 6·439; as issue in election of 1888, 9·667; and Latin America, 9·673; McKinley Act, 9·676; Dingley Act, 9·696; Payne-Aldrich, 10·771; Underwood-Simmons, 10·788; Fordney-McCumber, 12·897; Hawley-Smoot, 12·938; and Trade Agreements Act of 1934, 13·989
Taylor, Glen H.: 15·1152
Taylor, General Zachary: commands army in Southwest: 5·381; in Mexican War, 5·382, 386; elected

President, 5·390; dies in office, 6·406
"Teapot Dome": scandal in Harding administration, 12·907
Tecumseh: Indian chief, 4·272, 282
Teheran Conference: 14·1093
Telegraph: invention of, 5·376; and development of service, 11·810
Telephone: invented by Alexander Graham Bell, 8·619; and growth of services, 11·810
Teller, Edward: 15·1175
Telstar: communications satellite, **16**·1242
Temperance movement: 5·395
Tennessee: becomes sixteenth state, 3·212
Tennessee Valley Authority (TVA): created, 13·975
Tenure of Office Act: limits Pesidential powers, 8·580; used to impeach Johnson, 8·586
Texas: migration and colonization, 5·351; wins freedom from Mexico, 5·351, 352, 353; becomes independent republic, 5·353; issue in election of 1844, 5·379; admitted to Union, 5·380
Textile industry: in New England, 3·188
Thanksgiving: first celebration by Pilgrims, 1·49
Thayer, Eli: 6·426
Thomas, General George H.: 7·545
Thresher: invention of, 5·345
Thurmond, J. Strom: 15·1153
Ticonderoga, Fort. 2·124
Tilden, Samuel J.: nominated for President by Democrats, 8·622; defeated in disputed election of 1876, 8·624, 625
Tilden, William (Big Bill): 12·936
Tiros I: weather satellite, **16**·1226
Titanic: sinking of, 10·778
Tito, Marshal: breaks with Stalin, 15·1144; signs pact with Russia, 15·1192
Titov, Gherman S.: Russian orbits earth seventeen times, **16**·1239 6·406
Tobacco: 1·36, 1·45
Tocqueville, Alexis de: 5·347
Tojo, General Hideki: 14·1068, 1102, 15·1145
Tompkins, Daniel D.: elected Vice-President, 4·295; reelected, 4·304
Tom Thumb: first locomotive, 5·334
Toussaint L'Ouverture: 3·234
Townsend, Doctor Francis E.: 13·1006
Townshend, Charles: enforces English taxation, 2·110
Townshend Acts: apply new taxes on colonists, 2·110; repealed, except for tea, 2·113
Trade Agreements Act: provides for reciprocal tariff agreements, 13·989
Travis, William B.: 5·351, 352
Treasury Department: established, 3·187
Treaty of Ghent: brings peace with England, 4·290; and Great Lakes

disarmament, 4·297
Treaty of Kanagawa: with Japan, 6·425
Treaty of Paris (1763): ends French and Indian War, 2·99
Treaty of Paris (1783): ends Revolutionary War, 2·154
Treaty of Paris (1898): ends war with Spain 9·705
Trent affair: 7·500
Triangular Trade: colonial trade route, 2·107
Tripoli: declares war on United States, 3·230; defeated, 4·250
Truman, Harry S.: wins Vice-Presidency, 14·1100; takes office as President, 14·1108; at San Francisco Conference, 14·1109; at Potsdam Conference, 14·1113; makes decision to use A bomb in Japan, 14·1114; and price controls, 15·1131; acts in labor strikes, 15·1133; proclaims Philippine independence, 15·1134; and Truman Doctrine, 15·1137; recognizes Israel, 15·1146; signs Displaced Persons Bill, 15·1148; and loyalty investigations, 15·1151; wins Presidency, 15·1153; launches Fair Deal and Point Four Programs, 15·1154; announces Soviet atomic bomb, 15·1158; orders American forces to Korea, 15·1162; confers with MacArthur on Korean War, 15·1165; recalls MacArthur, 15·1166; in Korean War "Great Debate," 15·1167; orders steel plants seized, 15·1174; not a candidate for re-nomination 15·1176
Truxton, Captain Thomas: 3·216
Tubman, Harriet: abolitionist leader, 6·411
Tugwell, Rexford G.: 13·969, 1014
Tunney, Gene: 12·915
Turkey: and Truman Doctrine, 15·137
Turks: capture Constantinople: 1·8
Turner's Rebellion: Negro insurrection in Virginia, 5·336
Tweed, William Marcy: 8·603
Tweed Ring: 8·603
Tydings-McDuffie Act: 13·986
Tyler, John: opposes Bank of United States, 4·269; elected Vice-President, 5·365; becomes President, 5·367; and Dorr's Rebellion, 5·372; and annexation of Texas, 5·380; at southern peace conference, 7·490

U

Underground railway: assists runaway slaves, 5·336, 6·408, 411
Underwood-Simmons Tariff Act: lowers duties, 10·788
Union of Soviet Socialist Republics: see Russia
United Mine Workers: in strike of 1902, 10·740; in strike of 1919,

11·865
United Nations: created, 14·1109; Charter of, 14·1111; holds first meeting, 15·1130; in Korea, 15·1162; and International Atomic Energy Agency, 15·1193; in fifteenth session, 16·1234
United Nations Relief and Rehabilitation Administration (UNRRA): 15·1135
United States Housing Authority: created, 13·1015
United States Shipping Board: and wartime fleet, 11·838
Unknown Soldier: buried at Arlington National Cemetery, 12·896
USO: 14·1073
Utah: popular sovereignty in, 6·408; settlement by Mormons; 6·451
U-2 Spy plane incident: **16**·1227, 1228

V

Vaca, Alvar Nunez Cabeza de: 1·26
Valentino, Rudolph: death of, 12·915
Valley Forge: Washington's winter quarters, 2·141, 144
Van Buren, Martin: in Eaton Affair, 5·335; elected Vice-President, 5·340; elected President, 5·358; issues neutrality proclamation, 5·361; defeated for reelection, 5·365; nominated by Free Soil Party, 5·390
Vandenberg, Arthur H.: 15·1130
Vanderbilt, Cornelius: 6·432
Van Fleet, General James A.: 15·1137
Vanguard I: American satellite, 16·1213
Van Rensselaer, General Stephen: and Niagara campaign, 4·275, 277
Vanzetti, Bartolomeo: trial and execution of, 12·919
V-E Day: 14·1110
Venezuela: 9·709, 10·744
Vera Cruz, Mexico: founded by Cortez, 1·24; occupied by Marines, 10·791
Vergennes, Comte Charles de: and French-American alliance, 2·145
Vermont: and Green Mountain Boys, 2·124; becomes fourteenth state, 3·212
Verrazano, Giovanni da: 1·25
Versailles, Treaty of: presented to United States Senate, 11·861; includes League of Nations, 11·861; rejected, 11·864
Vespucci, Amerigo: 1·19
Veterans Bureau: created, 12·904
Vicksburg, Battle of: 7·523
Vicksburg convention: 6·454
Viet Minh: 15·1182
Viet Nam: 15·1182; 16·1250, 1261
Vigilantes: in California, 6·412
Villa, Francisco (Pancho): 11·815, escapes capture, 11·820
Vinson Naval Act: 13·1021
Virginia: Confederate ironclad engages Monitor, 7·505
Virginia Colonies: Roanoke, 1·36; Jamestown, 1·39, 41; women in, 1·44; Negro workers, 1·45

V (contd.)

Virginia Company: grants land to Pilgrims, 1·47

Virgin Islands: purchased by United States, 11·827

Virginius incident: rebel arms ship seized by Spaniards, 8·612

Vishinsky, Andrei Y.: 15·1158

V-J Day: 14·1115

Volstead Act: provides enforcement for prohibition, 11·857

Vostok I: Russian space capsule orbits earth, 16·1235

Vostok II: orbits earth seventeen times, 16·1239

W

Wade-Davis Bill: for reconstruction of the South, 7·535, 8·571

Wagner, Robert F.: 13·978

Wagner-Steagall Act: 13·1015

Wainwright, General Jonathan: 14·1071, 1115

Waite, Davis H.: 9·688

Wakarusa War: in Kansas, 6·431

Waldseemuller, Martin: names New World, 1·19

Walker, Major General Edwin: 16·1249

Walker, Robert J.: 6·438

Walker, General Walton H.: 15·1166

Walker, William L.: 0·432

Wallace, Henry A.: administers Agricultural Adjustment Act, 13·974; elected Vice-President, 14·1060; dropped by Democrats, 14·1100; dismissed from Cabinet, 15·1136; in 1948 election, 15·1152, 1153

Wanghia, Treaty of: 5·378

War debts question: complications after World War I, 12·903, 929, 944; and default in payments, 13·987

War Hawks: 4·271

War Industries Board: in World War I, 11·839, 843

War Labor Disputes Act: 14·1088

War Manpower Commission: 14·1072

War of 1812: declared, 4·273; causes, 4·255, 257, 260-262, 264-5, 267, 270-272; battles, 4·275-283, 286-290; peace negotiations, 4·284, 290

War Production Board: 14·1072

Warren, Earl: 15·1152, 1184

War Shipping Administration: 14·1075

Washington, George: in French and Indian War, 2·93-94, 96; background, 2·126; chosen commander of colonial forces, 2·127; fights in New York and retreats to Pennsylvania, 2·135; crosses Delaware River and wins at Trenton and Princeton, 2·138; at Valley Forge, 2·144; receives surrender of Cornwallis, 2·151; resigns as commander, 2·154; chairman of Constitutional Convention, 3·177; elected first

President, 3·184; inaugurated, 3·185; delivers first annual address, 3·189; approves United States bank, 3·194; relieves St. Clair of command, 3·198; refuses military aid to France, 3·201; reelected, 3·204; role in Whiskey Rebellion, 3·205; Farewell Address, 3·211; appointed army commander, 3·216; death of, 3·222

Washington, George C.: 6·418

Washington, D.C.: burned by British, 4·288

Washington Conference (1921-1922): meeting of powers on naval disarmament and Far Eastern matters, 12·895; results of, 12·918

Washington, Treaty of: 8·602

Watauga River settlements: 3·170

WAVES: 14·1084

Wayne, General Anthony: 3·206

Weapons: of World War I, 11·849

Weaver, James B.: leads Greenback Labor Party, 8·629; in election of 1880, 8·635; as Populist candidate, 9·678; and election of 1892, 9·682

Webster, Daniel: opposes Bank of United States, 4·294; in Supreme court cases, 4·302; champions federal supremacy, 5·331; debates with Calhoun, 5·342; nominated for President, 5·358; and Creole affair, 5·369; and Webster-Ashburton Treaty, 5·374; pleads for Union, 5·396; and Lopez affair, 6·413; and Hungary, 6·414; in 1852 election, 6·419; death of, 6·421

Webster, Noah: 4·313

Webster-Ashburton Treaty: settles American-Canadian boundary, 5·374

Wedemeyer, General Albert C.: 15·1159

Weld, Theodore: 6·411

Welles, Gideon: appointed Secretary of Navy, 7·491; strengthens Union navy, 7·494

Welles, Orson: and spectacular radio broadcast, 13·1026

Wesley, John: 2·91

West, Benjamin: artist, 2·106

West Florida: annexed, 4·268

West Point: established, 3·233

Weyler, General Valeriano: in Cuban revolt, 9·697

Wheeler, Burton K.: 13·1010

Wheeler-Howard Act: encourages tribal life among Indians, 13·990

Wheeler-Lea Act: provides controls over food, drugs and cosmetics, 13·1022

Whig Party: formation of, 5·344; in election of 1848, 5·390; in 1852 election, 6·418, 422; in 1856 election, 6·437

Whiskey Rebellion: 3·205

Whiskey Ring: scandal in Grant's administration, 8·616

White, Edward H.: walks in space, 16·1259

White, Henry: 11·856

White, John: 1·37

Whitfield, John W.: 6·427

Whitman, Marcus: on Oregon Trail, 5·355; massacre of, 5·388

Whitman, Walt: poet serves as nurse, 7·544; on political corruption, 8·607

Whitney, Eli: invents cotton gin, 3·203; inventions launch industrialization in America, 3·228

Whitney, William C.: 9·661

Wickersham, George W.: and prohibition enforcement, 12·941

Wigglesworth, Michael: 1·72

Wilderness Campaign: of Civil War, 7·532-533

Wilhelm II: German emperor, 10·744, 745, 756, 793; abdicates, 11·854

Wilkes, Captain Charles: and Trent affair, 7·500

Wilkinson, James: 3·174, 4·283

William and Mary College: founded, 1·72

Williams, Jonathan: 3·233

Williams, Roger: founds Rhode Island, 1·55

Willkie, Wendell: defeated in election of 1940, 14·1060

Wilmot Proviso: and slavery in new territories, 5·384

Wilson, James: 3·177

Wilson, Woodrow: nominated by Democrats, 10·779; elected President, 10·780; outlines Presidential policy, 10·785; tariff program, 10·788; declares American neutrality in World War I, 10·793; and Mexico, 10·790-791; moves against trusts, 10·795; acts in Lusitania matter, 11·813; urges preparedness, 11·816; reelected, 11·825; proposes "peace without victory," 11·828; announces break with Germany, 11·829; vetoes immigration curbs, 11·830; decides for war, 11·835; submits Fourteen Points, 11·844; and German armistice request, 11·854; at Paris peace conference, 11·856; and drafting of League Covenant, 11·858; presents Treaty of Versailles to Senate, 11·861; takes fight for League to people, 11·862; suffers paralytic stroke, 11·863; recalls troops from Russia, 11·867; and election of 1920, 11·869; death of, 12·902

Winthrop, John: 1·51

Winthrop, John Jr.: 2·106

Wirz, Captain Henry: 7·555

Witch Trials: in Salem, 1·69

Wolfe, General James: at Quebec, 2·97

Woman Suffrage Amendment: ratified, 11·870

Women's Auxiliary Army Corps (WAAC): 14·1084

Women's Unit of Marine Corps: 14·1085

Women's Rights Convention: 6·411

Wood, Grant: artist, 12·935

Wood, Colonel Leonard: 9·701

Woodson, Daniel: 6·436

Wool, Captain John E.: 4·277

Workingmen's Party: 5·330, 8·628

Works Progress Administration (WPA) furnishes jobs to unemployed 13·994

World Court: 12·952

World War I: begins in Europe, 10·793; causes of, 11·808-809; and American involvements, 11·812-814, 816-817, 819, 821, 822, 828-829, 832; and United States participation in, 11·835-854; officially ends, 12·891; and war debts and reparations question, 12·903

World War II: begins in Europe, 13·1031-1036, 14·1048-1052, 1054-1056, 1058-1059, 1063-1064; and United States participation in, 14·1069-1115

Wright Brothers: and first successful airplane, 10·749

Wright, Frances: 5·330, 6·411

Wright, Frank Lloyd: architect, 12·935

Writ of habeas corpus: Supreme Court rules on Civil War cases, 8·579

Writs of Assistance: 2·98, 110

Wyoming: admitted as state, 9·668

X

XYZ Affair: 3·214

Y

Yale College: founded, 1·72

Yalta Conference: 14·1104

Yancey, William L.: 6·454

Yazoo lands: 3·209, 232, 4·268

"Yellow Dog" contracts: outlawed, 12·949

Yellow fever: and Philadelphia plague, 3·202; overcomes French in Santo Domingo, 3·234; and Spanish-American War, 9·713; and campaign in Cuba, 10·730; and building of Panama Canal, 10·760

'Yellow Press": in Cuban revolution and war with Spain, 9·697

York, Duke of: in New Netherland, 1·61

Yorktown, Battle of: surrender of Cornwallis, 2·151

Young, Brigham: becomes leader of Mormons, 5·387; in Utah, 6·451

Young, Owen D.: and war debt plan, 12·903; devises plan for German reparations, 12·929

Young Americans: and Manifest Destiny, 6·417; and Kansas-Nebraska Act, 6·427

Yugoslavia: conquered by Germany, 14·1059; breaks with Russia, 15·1144

Z

Zangara, Giuseppe: attempts Roosevelt assassination, 13·968

Zenger, John Peter: American editor; fights for freedom of the press, 2·90

Zimmermann, Alfred: and plot to bring Mexico and Japan into war, 11·832